The Louder I Will Sing

I'd like to dedicate this book to my children, Brandon, Harmony and Ruby-Lee, who I love unconditionally and are my purpose and driving force for positive change.

To the following souls, who are no longer with us:

Jason, aka Fox, a dear friend with whom I shared many highs and lows. He will always remain close to my heart.

Dale, who was sadly taken away at a young age.

Madelina, a school bestie, who I loved dearly.

Mama Blackwood, who in the absence of my birth mother nurtured me as her own and whose faith in God never wavered.

Roger, aka Roger Ramjet. My ride or die cousin.

Uncle Mervin, my mother's brother. Who was a role model that I looked up to – intelligent, kind and always smiling.

Ma, my maternal grandmother, the matriarch of the family.

My parents, who I honour, respect and love.

I'd also like to thank:

Maureen, who first helped me to formulate my thoughts and memories for this book.

Tom, for his assistance, dedication and attention to detail.

The Blair Partnership, for giving me the opportunity to tell my story.

The team at Little, Brown, for their expertise, professionalism and commitment.

My friends and community for their continuous support.

Lastly, my family for trusting me to tell our story and believing in me to lead in our pursuit of justice.

The Louder I Will Sing

Lee Lawrence

sphere

SPHERE

First published in Great Britain in 2020 by Sphere

1 3 5 7 9 10 8 6 4 2

A CIP catalogue record for this book is available from the British Library.

ISBN 978-0-7515-8104-1

Typeset in Bembo by M Rules
Printed and bound in Great Britain by Clays Ltd, Elcograf S.p.A.

Papers used by Sphere are from well-managed forests
and other responsible sources.

Sphere
An imprint of
Little, Brown Book Group
Carmelite House
50 Victoria Embankment
London EC4Y 0DZ

An Hachette UK Company
www.hachette.co.uk

www.littlebrown.co.uk

Preface

Dancing, always dancing.

It was always a special day when Mum brought home a new record. Music, especially reggae, was the soundtrack of my childhood. If the record player wasn't on, it was the pirate radio station. If it wasn't the pirate radio station, it was a cassette tape spooling round on a stereo or a ghetto blaster.

Mum was back from Brixton Market, the bulging plastic bags of food left forgotten by the front door. It was her new record that we all wanted to hear – me, my sisters Lisa, Sharon and Rose. Mum slipped the single out of its sleeve, gave it a twirl in the sunlight streaming through the front sash of the living room. As she put the record on the player and lowered the needle, I heard the tell-tale crackle that the record was about to begin.

A short opening roll of drums. Then clipped stabs of guitar against an endless bass that seemed to rise and fall with hypnotic, laid-back precision. Floating over the top, the featherlight female vocals began: 'I want to share your life . . .'

I looked at my sisters and grinned. 'Someone Loves You Honey' by J.C. Lodge was one of the records of the summer of 1982. Number one back in Jamaica, every time you turned on a radio in Brixton it seemed as though the same sweet lyrics and pulsating bass were there waiting for you. Transporting you for a few fleeting moments away from south London towards sunnier climes.

In front of the record player, Mum was starting to move. It was as though the richness of the reggae beat was rippling through her. Some people are born with a natural sense of rhythm. Mum was one of them. As she turned around, she gestured for the rest of us to join her. We didn't need a second invitation. Everyone was up on their feet, swaying and swinging in a circle around the coffee table.

As the song reached the chorus we all knew so well, everyone started to sing along. The louder I sang, the more Mum smiled.

After

One

It was a few days after my mum passed away in 2011 that my life was turned on its head for a second time. The first time had been in 1985, when I was eleven, and a dawn raid on our house in Brixton left her shot by the police and fighting for her life. That incident had triggered the second Brixton uprising. After the debris and destruction of that weekend had been cleared away, my family were left to pick up the pieces of our lives. For my mum, Cherry Groce, it was coming to terms with the fact that the shooting had left her paralysed, and facing the rest of her life in a wheelchair.

The second time began not with a bang, but with a whisper. I was back at King's College Hospital in south London, where Mum had passed away, to collect some paperwork. In a strange way, I was grateful for the bureaucracy that follows on from when somebody dies. It gave me something to do while I was still making sense of it all. I was thinking about the arrangements for the funeral and needed to get hold of the death certificate to set that up. There was a paper trail to follow – get something from the hospital, take that to someone else at the council, and then get the death certificate.

I was in the early days of grief, still coming to terms with the fact that Mum was no longer around. It was odd being in the hospital without her there; it felt that little bit different, that little bit emptier. I'd been so many times to visit Mum I knew the way to the ward by muscle memory. But this time, I headed in the opposite direction, downstairs, in search of a small office in the basement. I explained to the woman behind the desk who I was and what I needed. She gave me a small smile of sympathy and disappeared to look through the files. I waited. The fluorescent strip light hummed.

OK, she said, returning. Here you go. But she didn't hand anything over. Instead, she continued to read. Then she whispered, more to herself than to me: Oh, hang on.

She looked up. She said: There's a comment here. The doctor has written something. I'm sorry, but I can't give you these at the moment. He thinks this might need to go to an inquest.

An inquest? I didn't know what that was.

It looks like the doctor is asking for a post-mortem to be done, the woman explained. And then this will need to be referred to the coroner's office to decide how to proceed. I'm sorry. These sorts of complications are probably the last thing you want.

She tilted her head to one side and gave me another sympathetic smile.

There was plenty I had wanted to happen in my life; this really wasn't up there with them.

It turned out that my mum's doctor wasn't certain about what the cause of death was. Or rather, he was clear on the medical reasons why Mum died, but wasn't completely certain about what had caused them. The post-mortem was done by a forensic pathologist called Dr Robert Chapman and took place a couple of weeks later. When I got sent the findings, I read it at my kitchen table in fits and starts; a paragraph or two, then flicking forward desperately, hoping that my brain would soak all the information up without me having to properly digest it. Mums aren't bodies to be dissected. As part of the process, the pathologist removed a section of her spine to take away and analyse. As far as I know, that's still in a lab somewhere, gathering dust on a white shelf.

Reading the report was hard going. Chapman described how he found a succession of metallic fragments lodged in my mum's spine. These were fragments from the bullet fired by DS Lovelock back in 1985, which had become embedded. That wasn't a surprise: from the start, the medical advice when Mum had gone to hospital was that it was simply too dangerous to try and remove them all – any attempt to do so could cause further damage. The doctors took out what they could. The fragments that remained caused my mum pain throughout the rest of her life. A recurring, sharp, stabbing reminder of what had happened one September morning.

But what was a surprise was Chapman's conclusion. It was those fragments, he said, that killed her. It was those fragments that had caused her paralysis and paraplegia, and it was the paralysis and paraplegia that caused a urinary tract infection and bronchial pneumonia, and it had been the urinary tract infection and bronchial pneumonia that had caused more infection and acute renal failure that was the last straw. I had it in my hands: incontrovertible proof that, over two and a half decades after my mum had been shot by a policeman, his bullet had resulted in the end of her life. The pent-up need for action sat in my throat like a stone that was on fire.

He thinks it might have to go to an inquest, the woman in the hospital basement had said.

I didn't know how an inquest worked or what it could do, but I knew that I wanted it. The first Brixton uprising in 1981, the murder of Stephen Lawrence in 1993 – they'd both resulted in public inquiries. After my mum had been shot, there had been an internal police investigation, which led to charges being brought against the officer who fired the gun. But he'd been found not guilty, and no public inquiry had followed. Public inquiries have a habit of asking awkward questions that authority figures don't want to find themselves answering. As a family, we'd never had a chance to find out what really happened that morning all our lives were turned upside down. Would the inquest give us an opportunity to do so?

I had a friend called Anthony, who was a solicitor. Without him, I don't know how I'd have found out what I needed to do; how many other people have wasted chances because they didn't know the right person to explain that the chance exists? My solicitor friend put me in touch with a guy called Evans Amoah-Nyamekye, a lawyer who specialised in inquests. He told me that inquests are required by law if a death is unnatural or caused by violence. They are a fact-finding process to clarify four questions: who died, where, when and, most crucially, how. If the death is as the result of an action by a police officer, then a jury is required. It wouldn't be a court case – the jury wouldn't be able to find someone guilty; instead they'd have to answer the questions set out by the coroner. The role of the coroner, Evans explained, was crucial. As well as deciding on the questions the jury would need to find on, they decide the witnesses the inquest would call. Essentially, they were in charge of the whole thing.

I needed to find a way to convince the coroner to follow the agenda I thought the inquest should follow. As Evans described how that worked, I realised that this was not going to be simple or easy. But it was a chance to find out exactly what happened leading up to the moment that had changed all our lives. My chance to get Lovelock in the witness box. To get people to listen to what took place. To get Lovelock and the Metropolitan Police to finally face up to and accept responsibility for what they had done all those years ago.

I'd been waiting for over twenty-five years for that moment, without even realising it. The time was now.

Before

Two

If you arrived at Brixton by Tube in the mid–1980s, the first thing you'd hear was music. There was a record shop, Solo Records, nestled in a corner of the ticket hall in the Underground station. As you came up the escalator, you'd hear the thump and beat of the bass and drums. Welcome to Brixton. Even before you climbed the stairs out onto the street, you knew you were somewhere different, somewhere special. Somewhere I called home.

Like today, the high street was a wide, two-way thoroughfare called Brixton Road, which actually starts a mile and a half away to the north, at Oval, and stretches all the way to the heart of Brixton, where it meets Lambeth town hall. The town hall is a large red brick building wedged on one corner of a crossroads, with a white pillared entrance like an old-fashioned bank, and a long neck of a clocktower that casts shadows throughout the day over the residential and shop-lined Acre Lane to the west, the high street to the north and the Tate Library Garden – one day to be rebuilt and renamed Windrush Square – to the east.

If you turn your back on the town hall, you can walk down the high street, a row of shops housed in more tall red brick buildings, studded with white-framed windows, and incense sellers and socialist speakers and steel-drum players wave at you on the pavement. Back in the 80s, Ford Capris, Ford Cortinas, milk floats and red buses with the numbers and destinations on black screens at the front spluttered down the road, yet the noise of the market on your right would still hit you before you saw it. The world-famous Electric Avenue bent round to the left like a banana between the colourful awnings of home furnishing shops, and there you could buy yams, oxtail and saltfish – you still can today. In 1985, when I was eleven, I'd move through it with my mum, weighed down with bags, being stopped every five minutes by Kitty and Dawn and Delores.

How are the girls getting on? Kitty said to Mum. Turning to me, Lee, you're getting big now! as she ruffled my head.

Would you look after Lisa for me tomorrow night? Mum asked tentatively.

The shouts of the market traders would rumble over the rustle of plastic bags and the scuffs of shoes on tarmac covered in the city debris of newspaper leaves and cigarette butts. At the end of the avenue is a road running perpendicular, where you'll find the train station. On the Electric Avenue side were plenty of butchers with red puddles pooling along the pavement, and fishmongers pumping out smells of the sea, and on the opposite side were the arches, housing shoe shops, wig shops and record shops blasting out their tunes.

If you google Brixton, you might think the area marked on the map looks a bit like a human heart. There was a perception back then, particularly from people who'd never been to Brixton, that it was dangerous, but that was never my experience at all. It wasn't a suburb with white picket fences, for sure; you had to have your wits about you and there was gang culture – but it's easy to judge gang culture when you're in a world where you're respected and have easy access to opportunities.

What Brixton had when I was growing up, was community spirit. It takes a village to raise a child, and Brixton was the village that raised me. It was a culture infused with a Rastafarian influence. Bob Marley was a voice on the record players of most households, but the ideas behind his songs spread well beyond the music. People would greet each other by saying 'brother and sister'. We'd go in and out of each other's houses; your mum was just as likely to feed me and ask me what I was doing and where I was going as my mum was to you. Helping each other out was how it worked. When our telly wasn't working, we'd borrow one: Reggie was a family friend, a little old guy in glasses in his seventies, who lived on the nearby Cowley estate. We'd be sent round to his flat and come back with his black-and-white TV until ours was mended.

We moved to Brixton when I was seven: me, my mum, my older sisters Juliet, Rose and Sharon, and my younger sister Lisa. We lived at 22 Normandy Road, a brown-bricked terraced house that to a seven-year-old kid looked like something out of *Coronation Street* – a world away from the fourth-floor flat we'd been living in down the road in Vauxhall. We'd been moved on because the flats were being knocked down. There was a lot of redevelopment going on at the time. It felt like such a jump to be in a house – with two floors and a garden and our own front door, black in a white frame with a half-moon window above it – and my mum filled it with music.

As you went in through the front door, the living room was on the left. It was a through lounge. On the right was my mum's bedroom and next to that was the kitchen. We had dark burgundy carpets and magnolia walls. We had this sofa we'd squish on together to watch TV: a multicoloured fabric one, of reds, yellows and creams. A coffee table in dark brown wood with a burgundy leather trim. In the far corner was the dining table. The tabletop was glass; it was a bit loose, so if you weren't careful when you were eating, it could slide.

Mum smoked, as did my dad. Benson & Hedges and Embassy.

Even with the sash window at the front open, there was always that faint tang of cigarettes. That and music. Mum had a lot of vinyl and tapes, and there'd be records on the whole time, playing away in the background even while you were going to sleep. She loved reggae and soul: Al Green, Percy Sledge, Randy Crawford, Aretha Franklin, Marcia Griffiths, Bob Marley, John Holt. They seeped into the walls.

Mum was very much in charge of the household: she cooked, cleaned and made all the decisions. Mine and Lisa's dad lived with his brother, also in Brixton, but we only saw him on weekends. Every Friday at six he'd appear at the door – sweets, crisps or fruit in hand – and stay until Sunday. He'd cook us a traditional West Indian Sunday meal before he left. A cooked-down stewed chicken, curried goat or some sort of beef, like oxtail. Every pocket of the house would fill with the smell of it, my mouth would be wet before I got to the table. Our week's food was defined by Mum's benefits. She got them on a Monday, so by Saturday we'd be on corned beef, liver or soup.

Dad had been in the army when he was younger, and now he was a security guard, but 'Dad' was never really a role he settled into. He made us call him by his name: Leo. One night, when we were still living in Vauxhall, Lisa and I stood giggling waiting for him to arrive, determined we could change his mind just by doing it.

Today, when he comes, I said to Lisa, we're just going to call him Dad.

I remember watching the clock tick down, the anticipation as six o'clock approached.

Right on time, he walked through the door and we jumped on him.

Dad! I shouted.

Dad! Lisa repeated as we hugged him. He put us down.

Oh, no. No, no, no. Just call me Leo.

I've never forgotten how that felt. I was heartbroken. He didn't want to be the person I wanted him to be. Later, my mum sometimes hinted that he had never really wanted children. It was something that had happened, but not something that he actually chose. Maybe his attitude followed on from that. He hadn't wanted to be a father, and so wasn't going to behave like one now.

Each Monday at school, we'd sit at our desks and the teacher would get us to do a writing exercise called 'Weekend News'. You took a piece of paper, you folded it into three, and in each section you wrote about Friday, Saturday or Sunday. And every Monday I would make up something that I wished my dad had done with me: taken me and Lisa out or built something or played a game with us. Because he never took us out, not once. Not even down to the park. My main memories of him are reading the newspaper, watching the television or drinking. Sometimes he'd turn up drunk on those Fridays me and Lisa waited so hungrily for, and you never knew who he was going to be when that happened. I don't remember seeing him hit my mum, but he could be physically aggressive, and sometimes she would get frightened. She'd pull us all out of the house and we'd have to stay with a friend until he'd calmed down. He often talked about the army when he was drunk — looking back, I wonder if he was suffering from a sort of PTSD.

After Mum died, he said to me, Your mum saved my life.

I asked him what he meant by that.

What woman would be in bed with a man, hear a noise and not nudge the man to get up and see what it was?

He knew that if he'd been the one to get up, he'd have been the one to get shot. He knew that because he was a Black man, and the police were looking for a Black man, he could quite easily have ended up dead.

*

19

Once, when I was about eight, I was asleep in bed when my brother Michael came over to Normandy Road. He prodded me awake and told me to come with him. It wasn't late, maybe nine or so. Mum wasn't there, but over at her friend Kitty's house; my sisters would have been watching me.

I don't have any shoes on, I remember saying sleepily.

He ignored that and gestured for me to follow him. He took me joyriding. I later found out the car had been stolen, but at the time I was so excited by it all, by the attention he'd given me. Michael was nineteen: he was eleven years older than me. He dressed different – he was hanging out with a group of white boys and tried to mimic their style in how he looked: Wrangler jeans, T-shirts, Gola trainers. Probably part of me being excited by that attention was because, like my dad, he was never around much. When we'd lived up in Vauxhall he'd been in borstal for most of the time, and, even though Mum kept a bedroom for him at 22 Normandy Road, the only memory I have of him in Brixton was him helping us to move there from Vauxhall.

I don't remember the last time I saw him before 28 September 1985, but it could have been months.

Three

I had a sheriff's badge, a toy gun and a holster. *Starsky and Hutch*, *Kojak*, *CHiPs*, *Hawaii Five-O* was my world. *The Professionals* had finished a couple of years before but that had been the best of the lot: a young Martin Shaw with a perm as the thoughtful but hot-tempered Raymond Doyle, and Lewis Collins as the confident tough guy William Bodie, solving crimes as they drove around in their silver and gold Ford Capris.

I could twirl my gun on my finger. I could run around the house, playing make-believe, catching the bad guys.

What do you want to be when you grow up, Lee? the adults would ask.

I want to be a police officer, I would say.

In September 1985, I'd just started secondary school and boy, had I been excited. Primary school had sometimes been tough. When we'd moved from Vauxhall to Brixton I'd had to change schools, and it was hard to fit in with the friendship groups that had already formed. There was a group of boys who called themselves the Panthers that I was desperate to get in with. The leader was a guy called Jimmy T: he was tall for his age, with a chipped front tooth and an afro. He'd always have a couple of afro combs with him, one with a pair of red and green handles you squeezed together, the other with a handle in the shape of a fist. Black Power.

You had to do initiation tasks before the Panthers let you in. If you want to join our gang, then you have to look at the sun until it burns your eyes, they told me.

The boys called themselves the Panthers because they all wore the same black Panthers trainers. Panthers were similar to Adidas, but while Adidas trainers had three stripes, Panthers had four. I begged my mum to get me a pair, so I could fit in, but when she finally relented and had saved up the money, the ones she got me were blue rather than black, and had Velcro rather than laces. The boys took one look at them and laughed at me. They told me they were the wrong sort of Panthers. That was how it was. I didn't get in.

Secondary school would be different. Stockwell Park was a huge school – about a thousand kids – and it didn't have a great reputation, but I had a couple of friends from primary school who were going as well, and I couldn't wait to wear the uniform. I know. That sounds a strange thing to say. What was even stranger was that the school didn't actually have a proper uniform. In the first few years, you just had to wear clothes in the school colours – lots of grey and blue. By the time I was fourteen, I was wearing whatever I wanted. I went to school in baggy jeans and a yellow padded jacket.

But when I started, I was keen to wear the full kit because I liked the idea of being smart. My dad had this black clip-on tie, so I borrowed that and wore it to school! I must have been one of the few kids there bothering. But it made me feel big and grown up, and so that's what I wore.

By Friday 27 September, I was beginning to settle in. I can't remember much of those first couple of weeks, to be honest. Everything that happened afterwards has left that a bit of a blur.

But I think I was getting my head round being somewhere new, somewhere different. I'd gone from being in the top year at primary school to being the youngest kid in the entire secondary school, because of my late-August birthday. It was all quite tiring and I was ready for the weekend.

In the early 80s, you only needed one thing to be cool: a BMX. They were expensive, so at first I'd tried to build myself one from bits of scrap bikes and broken parts I'd found. I had a frame from one bike, handlebars from another, a wheel from somewhere else. I fitted it all together but I didn't have any tyres so I was just riding on the rims – you could hear me coming a mile off.

Mum felt sorry for me, so she'd begged my dad to buy me one for my tenth birthday. He just said, When I was in Jamaica, we were riding donkeys.

But my mum persisted and eventually he gave her the money – £25 to buy a second-hand BMX from my sister's friend. For all my dad's protestations, my mum once caught him riding it himself.

See? she said. You didn't want to buy the boy the bike and now look at you, riding on it like a big kid.

I loved that bike. It was a Super Burner, which at the time were usually gold in colour, but you'd strip that back to the chrome. I had these yellow Skyway Mags wheels. I customised it, put a number plate on it, these little mushroom-like grips as well (for those who don't know their BMXs, these were a thinly ribbed, plastic design that you put on your handlebars, giving you a bit more grip and making them easier to hold).

I'd spent the summer of '85 at the bowlers, as we called them, five minutes from our house, round the back of the nearby community centre. Everyone on their skateboards, rollerskates and BMXs would go there to try out tricks. I wasn't the best, but I was pretty good: I could jump over a stack of tyres if I'd built up enough speed from starting at the top of the track. I'd nailed bunny hops, 180 spins, riding backwards. That's what I was going to do all weekend; take my bike to the bowlers, or up to the ones in Stockwell a mile down the road, and try out something new.

At six, my dad arrived as usual. Mum's friend Jennifer stopped by – she was going out and Mum said she'd watch Jennifer's two children, Shane age two and Sabrina age seven. It was a typical Friday night of music and TV. There was *Soul Train* on Channel 4, game shows like *Play Your Cards Right* and dramas like *Dynasty*. We used to watch the TV until closedown. In those days, TV didn't run through the night but would stop about midnight. They'd play the national anthem, and then you'd get this white dot on a black screen, a loud, high-pitched '*eeee*' to remind anyone who'd fallen asleep to switch the television off. Lisa and Jennifer's kids had nodded off, so we left them there on the sofa. The rest of us went to our beds.

Mum, my dad, Sharon and me all shared the same bedroom downstairs. That was off to the right as you came into the house. It had been that way when we'd had less rooms back in Vauxhall and so we were used to sharing. Mum had let my sisters have the other bedrooms upstairs, and kept one spare for Michael in the hope he'd visit. I liked us all being in the same room; it felt safe, like something from *Charlie and the Chocolate Factory*. My older sister Juliet, who was six months pregnant at the time, was upstairs in her room.

We were having a bit of an Indian summer. It was a warm night. Everything was still.

Mum, my dad, Juliet, Sharon, Lisa, me, the two kids. There were eight of us in the house. My sister was pregnant. Five of us were children.

Four

Bang.
  I didn't open my eyes, but my ears woke up. There had been a thump, a jolt. One of those quiet, early morning moments where any sound at all echoes out.

I felt Mum peel back the covers next to me. Semi-conscious, I thought it was probably Juliet doing something or other. Mum would find out. She was the lioness; we were her cubs.

BANG.

This noise was different. Louder, closer, sharper – I sat up, *jumped* up. I knew what that one was. A gunshot.

The door to the hallway was open and my mum was lying on the floor, a white man I didn't know towering over her, a gun in his hand. Her body was turned; she was faced more towards us than to him – she'd seen the man and tried to turn around to come back into the bedroom.

My instinct was fury. I jumped out of the bed, I screamed, over and over, What the fuck have you done? You shot my mum! You fucking shoot my mum again and I'm going to kill you!

Somebody had better shut this fucking kid up, the man with the gun said.

My dad was next to me. In a quiet, calm voice he said, Lee. Lee, calm down.

I looked up at him. In the blue light of the morning I saw fear on his face. He looked terrified. My dad, *my dad* – someone who'd been in the army, someone who worked as a security guard – was scared.

Noise suddenly rushed in everywhere, as if someone had unmuted a TV. More voices, dogs, more armed men appearing. Someone was shouting, Where's Michael Groce?

And then it struck me. In the middle of that hot pot of boiling-over rage, terror, confusion and noise, I realised they were police officers. The man who'd shot my mum was a policeman. It didn't make sense, none of it did. I was fully awake and in a dream at the same time. *Is this for real? Is this actually happening?*

Mum was wheezing on the floor, her face creased with pain, with worry. I can't breathe, she kept saying. I think I'm going to die. I can't feel my legs.

The bullet had gone through her shoulder, travelled down into her back, hit her spine, and come out the other side. But we didn't know this at the time.

I'd been ushered out of the room after my dad told me to calm down. But I'd fought my way back in. I wanted to go over to her. But with the policeman there, I couldn't.

It's just a graze, the policeman said. She's just got a graze, that's all.

I pointed to the dark patch of blood that had appeared out of her side.

So why is she bleeding? I asked.

26

After

Five

In the months after the death of my mum in 2011, there were various meetings between all the involved parties regarding the set-up of the inquest. Both the inquest and the meetings took place at Southwark Coroner's Court, which deals with cases across south London. It's nestled away behind Borough High Street, not far from the Thames. The Coroner's Court looks modern, with its timber-clad front, but has a history that goes way back.

I was in a grey suit with a white shirt. I'd driven my cab there and parked up in a taxi rank, shaking my head when someone asked for a ride. My heart was drumming a fast and hard beat. I was nervous.

The meeting room was a big boardroom, sliced down the middle by a large table where everyone else was already sitting. Between the coroner and the separate barristers representing the police forces involved – the Metropolitan Police, Hertfordshire Police Force – and those representing Inspector Lovelock, there were a lot of people. Thick files of notes sat in front of each of them, all primed to fight their particular corner.

And then there was me.

I couldn't persuade any of my family to come with me. I'd desperately wanted my mum's brother Danny to come, but

31

he said to me, You know what, Lee? Your problem is that you've got expectations. You shouldn't have expectations, just intentions.

My brother's response was, You know you're not going to get legal aid, don't you? For cases like this, for people like us, it's just not going to happen.

It felt like a kick in the stomach. But that sense of disillusionment had precedent. Back in August 2008, musician Sean Rigg had died in police custody at Brixton Police Station. Rigg had mental health issues and, having been arrested, was restrained by a number of officers, later dying of a cardiac arrest. In March 2011, the DJ and singer Smiley Culture died during a police raid at his home – a 'self-inflicted stab wound' was the official cause of death. In Tottenham in August 2011, Mark Duggan was shot and killed by police on the grounds he was carrying a gun and was a threat. Duggan was not holding a weapon at the time of the shooting.

In each incident, the inquest process had proved inconclusive. To those of us in the community, the cases felt self-evident, the police behaviour damning, and yet nothing seemed to happen. Injustice after injustice. It was the same old story.

After Mum died, my Aunt Julie and my wife, Gem, went to the hospital to help dress her and prepare her body. I asked Gem to bring me back Mum's hospital wristband and a lock of her hair. I kept them in a small, sealed plastic bag, and I took them with me to the meeting. I couldn't blame my family for not having faith in the system, but I refused to think like that. Instead I concentrated on what I was fighting for.

The reason I didn't have a lawyer with me was because Michael was right: I hadn't been able to secure legal aid by the time of the preliminary hearing. Evans Amoah-Nyamekye said he couldn't come in with me because I needed a QC or a barrister, and that if he'd come in with me, just that once, then it would have looked

32

like I had representation and so preclude me getting legal aid. We'd been looking for someone who could represent the case pro bono but hadn't had any luck yet.

So that was my task: Evans had told me that I just needed to get the meeting adjourned. *Every time they ask you a question, just say you want it adjourned. Get the hearing stopped, buy yourself some time to get legal aid sorted.*

As I sat down at the long table, all the pairs of eyes followed me, sizing me up, or – rather – sizing me down. I imagined they were thinking, *Is that it?* It felt as if they'd wanted a heavyweight rival to fight with, and instead got me – this amateur, a rank outsider, had stepped into the ring. A couple of them made notes, looked at their phones. The only one who gave me the time of day was a female barrister who was part of the team representing the Met. She smiled and acknowledged my presence.

The coroner was a small, white, wiry, powerful woman – sort of a cross between Margaret Thatcher and Mary Berry – who was well spoken and to the point. She was in charge of the room. She looked at me shrewdly and said, Do you not have any representation with you, Mr Lawrence?

It felt like a criticism – as if she was telling me off, as if I was a thorn in her side and stopping the process running as smoothly and quickly as she'd like.

She started the meeting, and straightaway it was as if the table had been picked up and dropped in another country where I didn't speak the language. There wasn't any allowance for the fact that I had no legal training, and there was a lot of discussion going back and forth that I didn't seem to be involved in. Evans's voice was replaying in my head: *Just say you want it adjourned.* I plucked up the courage and found myself clearing my throat and raising my hand to try to get attention.

The coroner turned to me. Mr Lawrence?

There was that stern look again. My throat felt dry.

I, er, I think maybe we should adjourn this meeting until the family have got legal aid and we have someone to represent us.

If the coroner didn't like me before, she really didn't like me now. But I stuck to my guns, dead-batting everything that came my way, on every point asking to come back on that when I had representation. I knew I was pissing people off – the other lawyers clearly just wanted it all done and dusted – but this wasn't a popularity contest. I had to hold my ground.

The one thing I did want to talk about was a police report Evans had dug up. In the investigations that had taken place after Mum had been shot, he'd found on record a question asked in the House of Commons in February 1987 by Stuart Holland, then MP for Vauxhall and our local MP. Holland had written to the Home Secretary asking that a report into Inspector Lovelock's role in the shooting be published, and he'd asked again about it in the Commons. The Home Secretary's response had been that if no charges were brought against Lovelock, it could be published, but then, because charges were brought against him, it had been decided that there was no requirement to release the report. On top of the report, there had apparently also been a memorandum of what disciplinary action was recommended. This was also never published.

I hadn't been aware that either had been done – there isn't a word to describe what it was like to find out that this material existed. On top of that, Holland asked further questions in the Commons about Lovelock's conduct, which I never knew had been in doubt.

He pointed out that 'unless the proceedings of the disciplinary enquiry are published, it will not be clear whether or in what way the Metropolitan police investigated, first, the claim that Inspector Lovelock had worked some thirteen hours the previous day on hazardous work including the use of firearms; secondly, whether later that day and on the evening before the raid on Mrs

Groce's home he had been drinking at the same strip club as the nine officers of the Hertfordshire force against whom disciplinary charges are being brought; thirdly, whether he admitted, or stressed either at the time or later during the disciplinary inquiry, that he had been drinking in that club, and that he did not wish to take part in the armed search of Mrs Groce's home for that reason; fourthly, how could it be, in such circumstances, that a request from a leading officer not to be assigned to the search raid early the following morning could have been refused by more senior officers; fifthly, whether those other officers insisted that he take part in the raid while being aware that he had been drinking and that this was in contravention of a Metropolitan police regulation that no officer should drink alcohol within twenty-four hours of handling a firearm?'

As I had read through those allegations, my eyebrows had gone up and up and up. The thought that Lovelock might have been drunk or had at least been drinking before he came into our house was abhorrent. There had never been any answers to Holland's questions, and I felt that surely the inquest was an appropriate time for that to happen and the report to be discussed.

So I brought it up and said we'd really like to see a copy of it.

The room went quiet and some of the lawyers shuffled in their seats.

The coroner asked, Why do you want to see the report?

I think it's important for the case, for us to see what those findings were.

Which findings?

I don't know, I said. I don't know what's in the report because I haven't read it.

I think we'd need a proper legal argument and justification as to why that report should be included before I could consider that request.

But we haven't seen the report, I argued. I can't tell you what's

35

important in the report until I've been allowed to read it. But if you need legal reasoning, then maybe that's another reason why we should adjourn this hearing until I have.

It was chicken and egg: until we saw the report, I couldn't tell the coroner why it was important; but I couldn't tell her why it was important until I'd been given approval to read it.

I was relieved when the coroner brought the hearing to a close, setting a date for when we'd reconvene.

As I left, feeling exhausted and drained, I noticed the various barristers were all chatting away to each other. I guess they probably knew each other from previous cases, but it reinforced my sense of isolation. A sense of them against us, the system against our family. I dragged my feet along the road, feeling deflated. Yes, I'd got the meeting adjourned, but I needed to get a lawyer to represent me next time or it would have been for nothing, and I was frustrated that from the off the coroner hadn't thought it was important for the police report on the shooting to be included.

Before

Six

Mum stayed on the floor where she'd fallen. The rest of us were rounded up and shut in the living room while the police officers searched the house from top to bottom; they must have thought Michael was hiding somewhere. Whatever information they were going off had been completely wrong – I don't know when he'd last been to our house.

I sat on the sofa alongside my sisters and Jennifer's kids, frightened and confused and terrified about Mum. I wanted to see her, but they wouldn't let us; they kept us contained. It was quieter now – less shouting, less barking – and I was tearful. We set each other off; pretty soon we were all sobbing. I was sat on my hands, rocking backwards and forwards, lost in my thoughts. What was going to happen to Mum? Was she going to die? No one could answer that, or say anything to reassure me.

Eventually, I heard an ambulance siren. I saw it drive up, and we stayed at the window, wanting to see Mum. The ambulance crew carried her out on a stretcher – she saw our faces pressed against the window. She rustled up a fake smile and was trying to wave at us, as if to say she was OK, even though she was clearly anything but.

And then she was gone, and my dad was too, and the original policemen – the ones who'd broken down the door, the officer with the gun who'd shot my mum – left as well. It was just us, stuck in a house now so turned upside down I wasn't sure it was ours any more, and a pair of young white female liaison officers. They'd been sent in to console us, look after us now that there were no adults left in the house. They were nervous, and doing their best to be reassuring. But we didn't know them, and it was one of their colleagues that had shot my mum.

Then a journalist showed up. A *journalist*. They let a journalist into our house. He started asking questions and wanted to take pictures. He lined us all up on the sofa and took a photo of us, even though we didn't want to and we were all crying. It was like something from a freak show, from a nightmare. It wasn't until years later that I finally saw the photograph: a friend of mine put together a set of news clippings about the incident, and there it was. All of our faces, screwed up and puffy, tears streaming down our cheeks. We looked like orphans.

We kept asking the liaison officers for news of our mum. They tried to hug us and stop us from crying, but they didn't seem to know anything either.

The news was playing in the background – I don't know why the TV was on. The liaison officers must have switched it on to try to distract us. Suddenly I heard the name of our street; they were talking about what was happening here. And then the reporter was talking about my mum. Our house, my mum – *this isn't real* – and then he said that she'd died from her injuries. Or that there had been reports she'd died from them, I don't remember. All I heard was the one bit of news I'd dreaded to hear. My mum was gone.

I was inconsolable, overwhelmed by the news that my mum was no more. I was crying, confused, out of control. I bolted to the kitchen, started opening and shutting drawers. I grabbed what I was looking for: a kitchen knife. If Mum wasn't around, what was the point of me carrying on? I didn't want to live. I pressed the cold edge to my skin. I gulped, took a big breath, and then one of the liaison officers appeared and snatched the knife away from me.

My mum was alive, she tried to reassure me. The story on the news was wrong.

I didn't know if I could trust her. The police – who were supposed to be the good guys, the ones there to protect us – had broken into our home; the news – there to report facts – was saying that my mum was dead when she was still alive? I wanted to believe the woman in front of me, but I was so distraught and exhausted, nothing made sense any more, and I didn't know if I should.

The woman pulled a pen out of her pocket. Hey Lee, have a look at this, she said, trying to calm me down. It was a novelty pen, a bit like a mini Rubik's Snake, that you could click flat into a pen, or fold round to make into a square. She handed it to me and I started playing with it, clicking it in and out of shape. I think I knew that she was trying to distract me with it, but that was OK, because I was in need of being distracted.

It's OK, she said. You can have that pen if you want.

It was a small moment, but an important one – in the midst of everything else, a tiny act of kindness.

Ours wasn't the only house with the TV on. Into all the pockets and crevices of the heart that Brixton covers, the news flowed like lifeblood, and anger began to beat.

Seven

What springs to mind when someone brings up the 80s? When I was living it, it was a time of BMXing, disco, funk, soul music, reggae, afros and the start of dub and bass, Jheri curls and jeans that came up to your waist. But with hindsight, it's hard to see it as anything other than a decade of struggle and strife. Margaret Thatcher, pit closures, unemployment at a record high, strikes, the IRA, AIDS, the Falklands, skinheads, the National Front and riots – so many riots.

I was too young to remember the first Brixton uprising in April 1981, although we moved to Brixton shortly after it had taken place. It followed on from a house fire at a property in New Cross in January, when thirteen people, mainly teenagers, were killed while at a birthday party. The claims by witnesses that a white man had been seen throwing something through the window were dismissed by police. Survivors described being interrogated by police as though they were criminals. No official message of condolence or support to the victims' families was offered (unlike after a fire at a disco in Ireland five weeks later, when both the Queen and the Prime Minister sent messages). 'Thirteen dead and nothing said' was one of the slogans used by campaign groups in the aftermath. Ten thousand people marched through London to show their support in early March. 'Day the Blacks Ran Riot in London' was the headline in the *Sun* the following day.

The Monday before the uprising, the local police had begun what was known as Operation Swamp. For a number of years, they had brought in the Met's Special Patrol Group, or SPG, to help flood the area with officers. These were stop and search tactics, the notorious Victorian 'sus' laws that allowed the police to stop people on suspicion of, well, whatever they seemed to feel like suspecting them of. It didn't take long for a clear pattern to emerge as to who was stopped and searched. Those stopped were disproportionately young, male and Black. The tactics eroded what little trust there was between the police and the community.

By spring 1981, the official liaison set up between the police and the local community had collapsed. The week before the uprising, Operation Swamp was in full flow, with the police failing to tell community leaders in advance. More than half of those stopped were Black; more than two-thirds were under twenty-one.

On the evening of Friday 10 April, a young Black man was running away from three Black youths when he was stopped by a white policeman. The policeman assumed that the man was running having done something wrong, and in the process of trying to stop him ended up tripping him and the pair fell over together. When the policeman stood up, he realised that he had blood on his uniform. He put a call out for an injured man. The man was spotted getting into a cab, where two policemen attempted to bandage his wounds. As a crowd gathered, the police tried to explain that they were trying to give first aid. The crowd, however, saw an injured man being stopped from going to hospital and a pitched battle ensued.

The following day, with rumours circulating that the injured man had died, Operation Swamp continued. Another police patrol stopped a Black minicab driver after seeing him put something in his sock. Despite the police officer's assumption that it was drugs, the sock contained what the man said it did – money.

The police officers then asked to search the minicab, but the driver was suspicious they might plant evidence, and refused. All the while, a crowd was gathering, as were police reinforcements. One of the officers was alleged to have an iron bar in a plastic bag; two other officers were spotted wearing National Front badges. Events quickly escalated into full-blown conflict – bricks, stones and petrol bombs were thrown by rioters. In total, 279 police officers and forty-five members of the public were injured, dozens of cars and police vehicles were set on fire, and twenty-eight buildings were torched. The next night, the same happened again.

More race riots were to come around the country that year: the Toxteth riots in Liverpool, the Handsworth riots in Birmingham, the Chapeltown riots in Leeds and the Moss Side riots in Manchester. These were all areas where racial minorities made up a large part of the community and where things were really tough. At the beginning of the 80s, the UK was in a recession, unemployment was high and inflation had sky-rocketed. The Conservative government's policies aiming to fix the problems were austere and hit these areas hardest. On top of that, new powers bestowed on the police allowed them to stop and search anyone they liked if they had 'reasonable suspicion' they'd committed an offence. The powers were applied excessively to Black people.

The tensions weren't new. They went back decades, to when immigration from the British Empire and then the Commonwealth had been encouraged to fill labour shortages left by the Second World War. The British Nationality Act of 1948 gave citizenship and permission to live in Britain to everyone in the UK and its colonies, and between 1948 and 1962 – when a new act restricted immigration – 170,000 people from the West Indies chose to move to what they'd always been told was their mother country.

The industrial towns of the Midlands was one area where a

large number of immigrants settled in the 1950s and 1960s. In five years in the mid-50s, the West Indian population in Birmingham grew from 8000 to 30,000; by the mid-1960s, Wolverhampton had a higher concentration of recent immigrants than anywhere outside London. In between Birmingham and Wolverhampton sits Smethwick, where in 1964 recent immigrants made up approximately 10 per cent of its population.

In 1964 tensions in Smethwick were already running high before the general election was called. The constituency was a marginal seat, and was a straight fight between Patrick Gordon Walker, the Labour MP, and the Conservative candidate, local headmaster Peter Griffiths. Griffiths's campaign was strongly anti-immigrant: campaign stickers and posters included the slogans 'Vote Labour for more nigger-type neighbours' and 'If you want a nigger neighbour, vote Liberal or Labour'. While Labour won the overall election with a 3 per cent swing, in Smethwick Walker lost his seat, with a 7 per cent swing to the Conservatives.

Then, on 20 April 1968, the Conservative MP for Wolverhampton South West and Shadow Defence Secretary, Enoch Powell, addressed the West Midlands Conservative Political Centre in Birmingham. The speech became known as the 'Rivers of Blood' speech, though Powell did not actually say those words. (He said, 'Like the Roman, I seem to see "the River Tiber foaming with much blood".') But there was plenty that Powell did say. He quoted one constituent, who had told him that 'in this country in fifteen or twenty years' time, the Black man will have the whip hand over the white man'. He told the story of another constituent who had written to him, a female pensioner whose street had been 'taken over' by immigrants: 'She is becoming afraid to go out. Windows are broken. She finds excreta pushed through her letterbox. When she goes to the shops, she is followed by children, charming, wide-grinning piccaninnies. They cannot speak English, but one word they know. "Racialist," they chant.'

The language was inflammatory and the evidence for Powell's arguments sketchy to say the least. A number of journalists attempted to track down the old lady who'd told the story about 'excreta' being pushed through her letterbox. Nobody could find her. Powell himself was evasive when grilled by David Frost in a television interview; the conclusion of many was that the tale was fabricated.

Powell was sacked from the Conservative front bench, and he was widely condemned by much of the media and the political class. Nonetheless, his comments found plenty of support elsewhere and he pushed his ideas further still. In November 1968 he called for a Ministry of Repatriation to help with the voluntary repatriation of immigrants. He quickly became the most popular politician in the country, winning the BBC's Man of the Year poll twice in the early 1970s. When the Conservatives won the 1970 election, many analysts suggested that Powell had helped swing power in their direction, his views gaining between one and two million votes for the party.

The effect of Powell's speech was to offer a cloak of respectability to those who harboured anti-immigrant and racist views. The year before his speech saw the launch of the National Front, formed from a collection of far-right organisations. Powell's views chimed with their strongly anti-immigrant message and one where violence was never far from the surface: 'White man, are you ready to fight?' the party's leader, Martin Webster, asked in 1974. There was a focus, particularly in late 1970s and early 1980s, of attracting football hooligans and elements of skinhead culture: 'A case of Millwall today and National Front tomorrow?' Webster was asked in a 1977 *Panorama* programme. 'We hope so,' he replied. That same year, at a National Front march in Lewisham, hundreds of Millwall football hooligans chanted 'Up the National Front! Kill the Blacks!'

Another organisation that flourished was the Monday Club.

They were a pressure group of Conservative MPs, designed to influence party and government policy. The group was set up in response to Harold Macmillan's 'Wind of Change' speech, which signalled the government's support for decolonisation (the speech was given on a Monday, which the group saw as a 'Black Monday' for people who supported their views). In the 1960s, the group's focus was imperialist; they wanted to save the empire. By the time of Powell's speech, they saw the way another political wind was blowing and they began to campaign more vigorously against immigration. In 1969, the group published a pamphlet called 'Who Goes Home? Immigration and Repatriation', which described the Race Relations Act as an 'engine of oppression', and, like Powell, called for a voluntary repatriation scheme.

By the early 1970s, the group contained thirty-five MPs, including six ministers in the new Conservative government, and an estimated 10,000 members nationwide. Such was the nature of the group's beliefs that in 1970, the Monday Club held a May Day rally in Trafalgar Square, at which a number of National Front members were present (the only difference in their repatriation schemes, really, was whether they were voluntary or compulsory). In 1973, the National Front leader John Tyndall was invited to speak by the Monday Club's Essex branch. The same year, the club ran a 'Halt Immigration' petition, describing immigration as an 'unarmed invasion' of the nation.

In April 1981, in the aftermath of the first Brixton uprising, the Monday Club called for the repatriation of 50,000 immigrants a year, offering an incentive of around £5000 to encourage people to leave. That October, the group's chair, Harvey Proctor, wrote an article called 'Immigration and Repatriation – Who Goes Home?' Echoing Powell's speech, he told of a case study of an old woman being attacked by a group of Black men while walking down the street: 'her fear is echoed by millions'. He blamed the Brixton riots on high levels of immigration. It was to be another two decades before the Conservative Party severed its links with the group.

In January 1978, with the Monday Club pushing for stronger policy on immigration, and with the National Front increasing their share of the vote, the Conservative Party leader and future prime minister Margaret Thatcher gave an interview to ITV's *World in Action* to talk about her views on immigration. 'People are really rather afraid,' she said, 'that this country might be rather swamped by people with a different culture ... the British character has done so much for democracy, for law and done so much throughout the world that if there is any fear that it might be swamped people are going to react and be rather hostile to those coming in.'

That use of the word 'swamped' felt deliberate – the fact it was used twice emphasised the point she wanted to get across. Thatcher was criticised for her comments: she 'knowingly aroused the fears of thousands of coloured people,' said the then prime minister Jim Callaghan, while others accused her of pandering to the National Front. But support for the Conservatives shot up after the television interview: in a subsequent by-election in Ilford North, the Conservatives took the seat from Labour while the expected support for the National Front collapsed.

You can follow this chain of comments further back or further forwards. At a cabinet meeting in 1954, the Cabinet Secretary noted that Winston Churchill said, 'Problems will arise if many coloured people settle here. Are we to saddle ourselves with colour problems in the UK?' According to Harold Macmillan's diaries, during a discussion on West Indian immigration in a cabinet meeting the following year, Churchill told his colleagues that 'Keep Britain White is a good slogan'. In 1958, when hundreds of white youths gathered to attack the West Indian community in Notting Hill, 'Keep Britain White' was one of the slogans that they shouted.

In the aftermath of the 1981 Brixton uprising, the government asked Lord Scarman to write a report on what had happened over that April weekend. Some of the report sounds every bit of its time – 'the British people watched with horror and incredulity at an instant audio-visual presentation on their television sets of scenes of violence and disorder in their capital city'. You got the sense Scarman didn't watch much TV.

But the report is a damning document. Scarman criticised the police tactics and the way they treated the local community. He said the force needed to be representative of the people it represented. He looked, too, at the social context – the lack of housing and education, and the employment issues that lay behind the anger and discontent many of those who rioted felt. It was a blueprint that offered a way forward. But the central recommendations weren't followed through. Twenty years later, when the Macpherson report looked into the murder of Stephen Lawrence, many of the same recommendations were made all over again. And in 1985, when the police launched that dawn raid that led to the shooting of my mum, little about underlying police attitudes or behaviour had changed at all.

The Windrush generation and other immigrants from Britain's colonies had been invited to Britain to fill labour shortages. They had come thinking they would prosper. Instead they were met with resentment and fear, and as the years went by, positive governmental policy was overshadowed by racist rhetoric, and they became the first to suffer when it came to economic downturns and the abuse of police powers. Knowing all this, it's not too difficult to understand why – having heard the stories circulating about my mum's death in September 1985 – a crowd gathered outside Brixton Police Station, chanting 'Murderers'.

Eight

Inside the police station, DS Douglas Lovelock was being interviewed under caution for having shot my mum. More people were joining the protest, getting angrier and more confident as it was swelled by reinforcements. The uniformed officers outside the station struggled to maintain control. Then a brick was thrown. A window smashed. Riot police, fifty of them to begin with, were deployed to try and restore order. Weirdly, they didn't try to say my mum was alive. Instead, some of the police officers in the station shouted back, inflaming the situation still further. Fuck off home, niggers, according to one account. A community leader and a member of the church tried to talk, but even as the priest was passed a megaphone someone in the crowd threw a petrol bomb at the front of the police station. The police and community leaders withdrew under a hail of bricks and stones. And that was when things really kicked off.

The media and the authorities described the events that followed as a riot. I see them as an uprising. I don't condone the violence, of course not. Once a situation like that flips over into violence and different people get involved, then the whole game changes, you know? The reasons why the thing began in the first place are lost in the rush and the mêlée and the situation becomes something else. Some people involved are plain angry and are venting their frustration in any way they can. Others are there to use the scenario for their own ends. It's a bit like a fire that has caught and can't be brought under control. Sometimes you just have to let it burn itself out. But I do commend the community for coming together and standing up as they did. If they hadn't, then my mum's shooting would never have been remembered in the way that it has. We as a family wouldn't have had the platform and the opportunity to revisit and reinvestigate what happened that Saturday morning all these years later.

I feel indebted to the community for that. I feel indebted to Brixton for the fact that they stood up for us. That wasn't easy. It takes courage to take a stand, especially when you know what the consequences and the brutality of the response were likely to be. There were people that weekend who got hurt or got arrested, ended up with convictions from their involvement, stuff they might not have done but they got sucked into the whirlwind of events and faced the repercussions as a result. The caricatures in the press about people being thugs or behaving like animals was a complete distortion of the motivations of many who were involved. They stood up for us, and I stand up for them for having done so.

I didn't know much of what had happened until Sunday morning. Saturday night, we'd stayed in Normandy Road, though it seems strange to think that now. The bedroom that I shared with my mum, Sharon and Lisa was closed off. I slept in the front room, we all did, with the liaison officers looking after us. That night was awful. Nobody could sleep. There was this ongoing melody of sobbing between me and my sisters. One person would start crying, then another, and another. None of us were really speaking to each other or consoling each other physically. We'd never been much of a hands-on, touchy-feely sort of family. That wasn't how we did things. And so we lay there, with the orange of the streetlight coming in from outside, each lost in our own thoughts.

I kept thinking about the word 'critical'. Every time I asked the liaison officers how my mum was, they said she was in a critical condition. Intensive, that was another one: still in intensive care. They used all those phrases you'd expect – she's in good hands, they're doing all they can, your mum's a fighter – all the platitudes. But the prognosis didn't change. My mum was critical. She stayed critical. And from the nervous glances between the two of them when I asked how she was, I could sense that they were unsure of what else to say. The words that I wanted to hear – *she's going to be OK* – were striking by their absence.

When I woke up the next morning, my friend Stephen McCalla knocked on the door and asked if I wanted to go for a walk to see what had happened. I wasn't sure at first, but he was insistent.

This all happened because of what happened to your mum, he said. You need to come and see it for yourself.

It was good to get out of the house. Even just briefly, to get away from what had happened. Sharon came with us, too. Stephen was slow walking – he was on crutches because he'd recently been in a car accident – but he was fast talking: Wait until you see this . . . you won't believe what's happened to . . . apparently the police . . .

I could smell the high street before I saw it. The smoke. The burning. There was this caustic stench that hung in the air, a bit like when you get a waft of a bonfire or a barbecue. But this smell was deeper, denser, more of a tang that gripped the back of your throat. That smell of man-made materials burning: metals, plastics. Next, there was a crunch underfoot. Glass. Shop windows that had been shattered, showered onto the pavements like shards of confetti. The sound of a shop alarm going off. Ringing and ringing and ringing against the stillness of the Sunday morning.

When I saw those streets, it reminded me of a war zone. A city that had been bombed in the war. London during the Blitz. There were buildings that had been taken out: burnt shells with steam and white smoke hissing out of them. Cars on their sides, or flipped over onto their roofs, black silhouettes. Some shops had their shutters half open, half shut, the metallic grilles twisted open like someone had attacked them with a giant can opener. Looking in, you could see the empty shelves, goods grabbed and discarded on the floor. The signs of makeshift weapons littered the street: stones, bricks, bottles broken in half.

There weren't many people around. It felt a bit like a ghost town, had this almost spooky eeriness to it. But there was an edge to it as well. You could sense the energy that must have pulsed through the place in the hours before. It's strange to describe – although the Brixton I knew had been transformed, what I saw didn't feel threatening to me. That was the difference between this and a war zone. We'd done this. Not somebody else. I was too close and too young to be able to really understand what I was seeing or articulate what I felt. It was the same with Stephen and Sharon. We could all sense the significance of what we were seeing, and I was glad that Stephen had taken me to witness it, even if I didn't yet appreciate exactly what it meant.

Now I can define it. A sense of belonging. Community. Power.

Nine

On Monday, we were taken to see Mum at St Thomas' Hospital near Waterloo. It had been the longest I'd ever gone in my life without seeing her.

We travelled there in convoy. Me, my siblings, my grandmother (who we were staying with); my uncles Mervin and Tony driving us. The hospital felt huge and bewildering – corridors and lifts and stairs going off in all directions. Arrows to departments with names I didn't recognise. The ever-present tang of disinfectant. We took a lift up and went along a corridor that felt as though it went on forever.

Mum was in a room by herself. The first thing I noticed was that she had a large box, draped with a white sheet, covering her legs. I was so pleased and relieved to see that she was alive, but the box immediately worried and confused me. That wasn't where she had been shot.

It was a tight fit in the room, with everybody squeezed in along the sides. I remember we all stood there awkwardly. No one seemed quite sure what to do. There were so many people in the way, I couldn't reach round and give Mum a hug. I just wanted to feel her and be close to her. I didn't like the box and looked away. Through the window behind, I could see Big Ben across on the opposite side of the Thames.

The doctor arrived.

I'm glad you're all here, he said. I can give you all an update on what the situation is. He glanced down at the clipboard he was holding and then back up. I'm afraid that Mrs Groce's injuries have resulted in paraplegia, a paralysis of the legs and lower half of the body. He was very matter of fact. I didn't know what those terms meant, but understood the simplicity of what he said next.

She's not going to be able to walk again.

The surgeons had operated on Mum with the aim of removing the bullet, but once it had entered her body it had fragmented and become embedded in her spine. That was the root cause of why Mum wouldn't be able to walk again. The doctors had taken out as many of the fragments as they dared, but they couldn't get them all out without damaging her still further, and risking her becoming even more seriously disabled than she already was.

My brain faltered. I couldn't wrap my head round what the doctor was saying; the words were like a wet bar of soap – every time I tried to grasp them, they slipped further away from me. *There must be a way*, I thought, *that she can recover and learn to walk again*. I had faith in God; I couldn't believe he would let this happen. He'd find a way somehow to help her get better. Surely. My mum was the life and soul. She was a dancer. Put the needle on a record, let the music fill the room and she'd come alive. She couldn't spend the rest of her life in a wheelchair, she just couldn't.

Mum didn't say much. She was conscious, propped up. But she looked tired, exhausted. She was deep in her own thoughts. My sisters and I were too. There was just the beep of the machine my mum was wired to, to punctuate the silence.

Ten

We were so loved. My mum was a rock and we clung to her, and she carried us uncomplainingly. But there were a lot of us, and as strong as she was, we must have been heavy. Money was really tight. She did cleaning jobs here and there. She'd do secretarial work. She'd also go down to the bookies with her friends, put a bet on the dogs in the hope of winning some money. She was good at it – the sofa, the carpet, they'd come from her winnings. She'd have a dream about this number or that number, and that was how she'd select which dog she'd put her money on.

But it was still tough. During the week, I was grateful for the food we got at school. It wouldn't be unusual for us to go without having had anything for breakfast. Those mini bottles of milk you used to get at morning break time, that was often the first thing I'd had that day. School dinners were completely different to what we ate at home: we'd be served the traditional stodge of the times, but I didn't mind that, even grew to like it. I'd get a full meal and a dessert, which I rarely did at home. I became accustomed to, and then got to like, that thick, lumpy custard that used to be slapped onto every pudding. I would go up for seconds and thirds if there was any left. Whenever I wasn't feeling well, my mum would say to me, Lee, you don't have to go to school. But I'd tell her I wanted to go. I wanted the school dinner, to get that one proper meal inside me.

I was aware of the struggles from an early age. I wished I was able to help. One day I said to my mum, When I grow up, I'm going to own a shop. And then you can come to my shop and take anything that you need.

All of this was before. What were we going to do now?

Mum had to stay in the hospital for the foreseeable future. Our grandmother lived a mile south of Normandy Road, off Brixton Hill between Brixton and Streatham, and it would have been too much for her to look after all of us – plus she was strict because of her religious beliefs, so we'd have gone mad at her house. So we were split up. A friend of my mum's, Monica, who was also Sharon's godmother, agreed to take me, Sharon and Lisa. She lived on an estate in the centre of Brixton – it was fun to be in the heart of the place, but the estate also had a reputation, which we had to learn to deal with.

The Somerleyton estate was known locally as the Prison, because of the way it had been tightly built and hemmed its occupants in. It felt a bit like one of the projects in America. There were walkways and alleyways to get around, and being jumped was always a risk as you walked through. The most notorious resident was a guy nicknamed Yellow Baby. He was a little guy with a big reputation. A tough nut. A fighter. Later, I got to know him, and actually he was pretty cool. But when I first moved in there, I followed the advice to keep clear of him.

Monica had children of her own – four of them – and like the rest of the flats on the estate, her home wasn't huge. I moved into a bedroom with her youngest son, Lisa and Sharon with her two daughters, while Monica's oldest son had his own room. To begin with, it was good to be there. Monica was more relaxed than my gran. There was music in the house again. And no rules about when we could watch television, either. Being back in Brixton

59

meant that it was easier to see people and to see Brixton as well. Monica was kind. Early on, I had to get a tooth taken out and she went with me to the dentist. The dentist was a bit old school, and clamped a mask over my face to knock me out. When I came round, dizzy and disorientated and emotional, Monica was there to comfort and support me.

But as my mum's stay in hospital extended, it soon became apparent we were going to be there for a while; in the end, about a year and a half. The atmosphere started to get tense. The son whose bedroom I was sharing wasn't happy that I was there – and in a way, why should he be? He'd had the situation dumped on him. We were so grateful to be there and not to be in care, with foster parents, but it was hard not to notice that Monica would buy things for her children but not for us. Sometimes we'd be given different stuff to eat, or they'd get new clothes and we wouldn't. Kids notice these things and that sense of not feeling wanted, of being treated differently, stung.

In the beginning, we'd leave Monica's and go back to Normandy Road at the weekend. Juliet was still living there. She'd had her baby – a boy called Aaron. My dad stuck to his old routine of being around from Friday evening until Sunday. It was strange to be back there. I didn't really enjoy it. It felt the same but different, if that makes sense. Where my mum had been shot, the carpet had been cleaned. There was no noticeable stain or trace of what had happened. But memories of what happened that Saturday morning would come back, as if out of nowhere. They were always swirling just under the surface. Sometimes I'd be quite jumpy – there'd be a knock on the door, and immediately I could feel my heart pumping away.

The thing I noticed most was the lack of music. When Mum was there, there'd be records spinning the whole time. Now, there was just silence. Without Mum, Normandy Road felt hollow. It didn't feel like home any more.

My dad remained the same through all of this. He was no more effusive than he'd been before the shooting. Even though Mum was in hospital, he didn't seem to feel the need to pick things up in her absence. Eventually Juliet was rehoused and left Normandy Road, and the last link to what had been home was gone. At the weekend, sometimes Lisa and I would go to my dad's brother's, Uncle Papa's. It was his wife, Auntie Bebe, who'd look after us. She'd cook dinner and we'd sit down to watch Saturday-night TV together. *The Price is Right. Family Fortunes.* At some point in the evening my dad would turn up, though again he wouldn't say much. This went on until my dad's brother's wife said that they needed to redecorate the house. They started doing that work and we stopped going.

For the first six months or so, Mum remained in St Thomas'. Every day after school, I would visit her, that was my routine. I'd get home from school, get changed. Sometimes I'd get a lift up from Charles, a good friend of my mum's who was very supportive. But usually I'd catch the 109 bus up to the hospital. I'd be there by about six or seven, and stay until about nine or ten. I remember that, a few weeks into this, Monica took me aside and said, You know, Lee, you don't have to go to see your mum every day. At the time, I almost felt offended by that, that it was as though she was saying I shouldn't be going. But I think she was more worried about me – that by doing this, I wasn't doing other stuff, childhood stuff, like hanging out with friends or doing homework. But for me, I didn't feel as though I had a choice. This was my life now. And it was my job to go there and look after her.

My mum would have a roll call of friends, family and neighbours coming through: quite often they'd be chatting away, and I'd just be sitting alongside, listening. Her friends would try to keep her in the loop about everything that was going on in

Brixton, gossiping about mutual friends and what they'd been up to. At other times, it would just be me and her. She was always keen to know how things were at Monica's, how I was getting on at school. Sometimes I'd turn up and she wouldn't be there. I'd initially panic. Oh, she's had to go down into theatre, someone would say. Because the nurses knew me, they were happy to let me stay in her room and wait for her. I'd lie down on her bed, breathe in her smell and kick back until she returned.

A large part of Mum's recovery was physio – building up her strength in preparation for when she'd eventually leave. I wanted to learn what I could do to help. I'd sit in on the sessions as they taught her about transferring weight, about how to move your body, how to use the wheelchair. Sometimes I'd get in the wheelchair myself, to try to imagine what it was all like for her. Sometimes that made Mum laugh – I learned how to do wheelies and would spin around in front of her. At other times, she didn't like seeing me in it. Don't jinx yourself, she'd say.

One time, early on, I remember being there sitting on the edge of the hard plastic visitor's chair, when I saw her leg move. *Did I see that right?* I thought. If she's feeling movement in her leg, maybe she will be able to walk again after all. Mum saw my expression, my hope, and let me down gently. It's just a spasm, she said. It does that sometimes. I can't control it. It doesn't mean anything.

I tried to alleviate her suffering. Those fragments of the bullet that remained lodged in her spine, they caused her a lot of pain – back troubles that she struggled with for the rest of her life. There'd be a lot of tension there as she tried to cope with it. I got increasingly adept at massaging her, knowing exactly where to work her back, to help ease the pain.

In spring 1986, Mum got transferred to Stoke Mandeville Hospital up in Aylesbury in Buckinghamshire. This was a hospital that specialised in spinal injuries and was the perfect place for her to go to continue her rehabilitation. But it meant that we saw a lot less of her, only going up at weekends. The social worker who drove us up had this bright orange Mini. She was a white woman in her mid-twenties, with curly hair that reminded me of Leo Sayer. At the time, there was a Whitney Houston song in the charts, 'Saving All My Love for You'. That always seemed to be on the radio when we were driving. Even now, when I hear that song, it takes me straight back to those journeys.

Stoke Mandeville was quite a different place to St Thomas'. Mum was with other people, all in wheelchairs and involved in their own rehabilitation programmes. That process was important for her to learn to be mobile and to be independent. There was more physio and building up of upper body strength, but there was a lot there about living too – simple things that you took for granted before, but had now become a difficulty. How do you get from your bed to the wheelchair in the morning? How do you cook on your own? How do you go to the bathroom? All that sort of stuff.

It was a different feel to St Thomas'. The view outside Mum's window was the green of the gardens rather than the Houses of Parliament and Big Ben. It didn't feel like a hospital in the same way. Unlike St Thomas', the patients were much more mobile: rather than being in bed, many were trying to move around. Everyone's situation was different. There were people there para-lysed from the neck down, who could only communicate by moving their head. That was hard to see.

In some ways, it reminded me of a prison: the fact that Mum was so far away from us, and we were only allowed to see her for visits once a week. When I went, I could see she wasn't happy. At St Thomas', friends would drop by the whole time. Here, she was much more isolated. The first time I visited, it struck me how white the place was – both the patients and the staff as well. My mum wasn't completely cut off. She struck up a friendship with Charlotte, a younger white girl, who was also learning to deal with being paralysed. They were quite different people, but they developed this odd-couple sort of relationship. Charlotte was confident and feisty, and always trying to lift Mum's spirits.

Each time we had to leave to drive back to London, it was hard to say goodbye. Mum was at Stoke Mandeville for the best part of a year. That was having spent six months at St Thomas' before that. Eighteen months of her life that she'd lost, and we'd lost as a family as well. And even when I was looking forward to her finally returning to London, I knew that it would be different to before. Her life – and ours – would never quite be the same again.

After

Eleven

I stood in the doorway of my living room while a crew of people set up cameras, lights and microphones.

Lee, what are you doing? I kept thinking to myself. But it was too late to back out now. I was going to do what it took – and if that meant leaving myself vulnerable and exposed on TV, then so be it. I'd got to this point because we were stuck behind a wall, and on the other side was legal aid. At the second hearing I'd found a barrister who was happy to represent me pro bono. John Cooper was this big white guy with crazy hair – a lawyer in the Michael Mansfield mode, in both looks and appearance. He asked to see a picture of my mum, and that seemed to fire him up. I'm going in there, he said. And he did: he took up the case for the police report to be included in the inquest.

The coroner took him a lot more seriously than she took me, but she didn't roll over to his demands.

The most I may be able to do is to let you see the report, she said.

The barrister continued to push. If the document was sensitive, he said, could it be arranged for us to see it in a room? So we wouldn't be able to take it away or make a copy or anything, but at least we'd be able to go through it and see what was in there.

That was where we got to when the second hearing was

adjourned. I left that session feeling a lot more confident that we were making progress.

But in the run-up to the third hearing I received a call from the barrister's office. I was told that Mr Cooper was not available to represent us at the next hearing.

I was crushed. I didn't have time to find someone else before the hearing. The coroner wasn't sympathetic.

We can't wait forever, she said. We will get to the point where, if you haven't secured legal aid and representation, we're just going to have to carry on with the inquest anyway.

The unfairness of that statement fired me up. She was essentially saying that the case could continue without us being properly represented, even though everyone else in the room was. Her implication was that we should trust her, that she would carry out her role effectively, and the inquest would reach the right conclusion. But I wasn't convinced that was the case; the argument over the police report was example enough that she wasn't willing to represent everyone's views equally.

In the third meeting, we went back to arguing over the inclusion of the report. Without the barrister there, it was down to me to make that case. I didn't have his learning or experience, but I fought as best I could. Every time the coroner tried to shut me down, I came back, refusing to take no for an answer.

And then the barrister for the Met spoke up.

Clearly, Mr Lawrence is not going to give up until he has access to the document, she said. Can I propose that to move this forward we do give him that? I'm prepared, on behalf of the Metropolitan Police, to make the necessary redactions and remove any sensitive information. We'll also need to take out names and addresses as required. But if that detail is excised, then I think we could be in a position to hand the report over for him to read.

My mouth fell open. The huge room hushed; the coroner and the other lawyers were just as surprised as I was. I felt a small flicker of hope, and a moment of triumph that the coroner's argument had been undercut. The other lawyers argued amongst themselves – each had their client's interest to represent and wanted that taken into account in terms of what information was redacted. But the main point had been conceded and it was satisfying to have got there just with determination and perseverance. It gave me the encouragement I needed for what came next.

And that was getting legal aid. We couldn't afford the legal support everyone else had come with. We'd applied for legal aid but that had been turned down flat. To appeal the decision, we needed public support to back us up.

I decided to put a petition up on the website Change.org, but I didn't have the first idea how to make it a success. It was easy enough to start, but how you went about persuading people to sign it in the sort of numbers you needed for anyone to pay attention – that was much more difficult. I had been a nightclub promoter, so I tried to use my experience from that: getting the word out, talking to the community. But filling a nightclub was one thing. Creating a successful petition was another. We tried to word it as best we could.

We are the family of Cherry Groce the innocent mother who was shot and paralysed by the police in 1985. Independent reports state that the events in 1985 were a significant contributory factor in our mother's death in 2011. An inquest is being held in June. But we've been denied legal aid, without it we can't afford a lawyer to represent us at the inquest and ask questions of the police.

Without legal aid we will be financially excluded from participating, which means we are not able to adequately and effectively take part in such a complex case and it is unfair to expect us to do so whilst the other three interested parties are being publicly funded!

71

Following the request of a revealing report we have received an apology from the police which comes 28 years after the shooting (and is still yet to be made in public).

One minute of your time will bring us closer to the answers we have been waiting 29 years for. Please sign to show your support in the fight for legal aid which will allow us a fair inquest.

I'd set a target of 10,000 signatures, which the rest of the family thought was crazy.

Why did you choose such a high target? they said. We're never going to get anywhere near that.

But there was no point getting less than 10,000 – we needed that sort of number for the government to listen. After a couple of weeks, between our family and friends and the local community, we'd managed to pull in 2000 signatures. It wasn't a bad effort, but I knew we needed to take it wider.

A year earlier I'd spoken with a journalist called Simon Israel, from *Channel 4 News*. It was just after the death of Margaret Thatcher, and Simon was doing a piece around various events that had happened in the 1980s. He'd contacted me to see if I'd be interviewed about my mum and the shooting. At the time, we didn't even know for certain whether the inquest would be taking place, and were just in preliminary discussions about it. It felt too soon to go on the TV and start talking about the case, and I explained all this to Simon.

That's fine, he told me. Whenever you're ready, just reach out to me and we'll sort something out.

I rang Simon and we arranged to meet at a branch of Caffè Nero in Crystal Palace. We talked it through. I said I was willing to go on TV, on the condition he helped with the petition – and he agreed.

So there I was, in my living room, with a camera crew alongside Simon, setting everything up. Gem was at work, but Rose and Lisa came with a couple of my nieces. The crew filmed us together, sat at the dining table in a group interview. The lights on my face were strangely hot and I felt vulnerable: the proverbial rabbit in the headlights. Then Simon and I went outside, and we filmed a one-to-one interview in the garden.

Are you ready? Simon asked.

I took a deep breath and nodded.

The interview both felt like it went on forever and was over in no time at all. Simon asked me about what happened back in September 1985, and why we needed legal support for the case, and I talked through it as calmly and truthfully as I could. After we were finished, Simon asked me carefully, How did you find it?

What he meant was, how did I find talking about something so personal to strangers? How did I find the thought of revealing myself on national television?

It was meant sympathetically but reinforced the enormity of what I'd just done. By the time the camera crew had packed up and left, I had a thumping migraine. I went upstairs and lay on the bed with the light off, praying I hadn't made a fool of myself. I hoped that I'd done Mum proud.

The interview was shot on the Tuesday and was shown that Friday evening. My sisters came round so we could watch it together, along with Gem and the children. It had been an agonising wait for it to run and I watched it, shoulders as set as a steel bar, on the edge of my seat. It was so strange to see myself on TV that I wasn't really able to get a sense of how it would go down. The rest of the family were warm and reassuring: What were you worrying about? See? You're a natural at this.

But even then, I wasn't sure. I knew they would be nice about it, however bad it was. I couldn't help noticing that I'd hardly mentioned the petition at all, and it had been down to Simon to mention it in his summing up.

The next day I was taking my son Brandon and his mum Debbie to look around some universities. Although we separated shortly after Brandon was born, Debbie is still a big part of my life and we're committed to the co-parenting of our son. We went up to the University of Hertfordshire in Hatfield. I was glad to have something specific to do, so that I wasn't just sitting at home staring at the petition. When I woke up that morning, the first thing I did was check how many people had signed. The number had grown from 2000 to 4000. The interview had done something, then.

As we walked around the campus of the University of Hertfordshire, every now and then I checked the numbers on my phone. Wow. That 4000 became 10,000, then 10,000 turned into 20,000, 20 became 30 became 40,000. Every time I looked, the numbers had jumped again. It was crazy. I showed my phone to my son and Debbie, and I remember him cracking this huge smile.

By the end of that first twenty-four hours, the number of people who'd signed the petition had gone from 2000 to 75,000. By the Monday, we had 130,000 signatures. I was truly humbled, touched that so many people had responded.

And people didn't just sign, they also wrote messages of support, explaining why they had added their name. Before that point, I thought that the only people who would understand the situation was the Black community, and maybe even narrower than that: the community in Brixton, and those who had suffered from police brutality and those sorts of injustices in the past. But people were signing the petition for other reasons, too, and from all over the country. For some people, the issue of legal aid was the trigger, the unfairness of people like us being deprived of support, while everyone else in the case – the Met, Hertfordshire Police, Lovelock – all had representation provided through public funding. We had a lot of signatures from lawyers, interestingly. Given my general experience with them, I hadn't expected so many to be on our side. There were others who signed because they'd looked at what the police had done and felt that the way we'd been treated was completely unfair.

It made me realise that our case was not as isolated an example as I might have thought. People from all over were rooting for us. That's a humbling thought – the number of people who weren't Black but were still connected to the situation. It made me realise that our story was part of something bigger, a wider issue. I can't express how much strength I got from that support. For the challenges we faced in the legal process, this was one of those moments when I felt, *yes*, maybe we can do this.

But the experience had taught me a lesson as well. I'd been so nervous about opening up when doing the interview, but here was proof positive that I could be myself and people would respond and react. After that, I became more confident about showing who I really was in public. It had helped me to speak up. I had found my authentic voice.

Before

Twelve

After a year or so at Stoke Mandeville, my mum finally came home – not to Normandy Road, but to a purpose-built bungalow on an estate in Gipsy Hill. It wasn't Brixton – we were three miles south now – but it meant that the family could come back together for the first time in eighteen months.

The bungalow was wheelchair friendly: it had decent access, proper facilities, the plug sockets were at a lower height, everything was on one level. So that was good. The estate itself was less so. The council seemed to treat it as a bit of a dumping ground for problem families. There were people there dealing with all sorts of issues. Drugs were pretty rife. I was adamant that I didn't want to move schools, and even though the journey to Stockwell Park was a long one, I continued to go there. That meant it took longer to get to know the other people on the estate, and that probably didn't help with how I settled in. But I was excited to be back living with my mum again. I felt as if we'd outstayed our welcome at Monica's house, and I was glad to be out of that atmosphere and the tension that had built up.

As soon as the house had become available, we were so excited that we moved in even before the furniture had arrived – we had a mattress for my mum, whilst me, Lisa and Sharon slept on the floor. The whole place smelt of new carpets. We had a celebratory meal, sat cross-legged in the sitting room with a big bucket of Kentucky Fried Chicken that we passed round between us. We had hot chocolate, too, with sweet milk and nutmeg. It was a good moment.

When my mum first came back, she was determined to be independent. She would vacuum in her wheelchair, do the cooking: she wanted to prove that there wasn't much she couldn't do. She had a standing frame where she could raise herself up with support. Her legs would be strapped into it, and she could stand there for ten or fifteen minutes, just to give her that sensation of standing again.

But as time went on, that initial enthusiasm started to decline. To begin with, she wanted to get out and see people. Soon after she was back, her friends took her out and somehow the wheelchair hit a kerb and she fell out. After that, when she went out, she would often prefer to stay in the car. Someone would drive her down to Brixton, but rather than going into the pub she'd sit in the car outside and people would come and talk to her. Part of it was that she was worried she might have a fall again. But part of it, too, was that she didn't want people to see her like that. After a while, she started going out less and invited people round to the house more. She was happier to create that atmosphere and environment there. She'd put all her old music on, bring out the food and drink – there were occasions when you could squint and it was almost like old times.

I loved those moments. But they were just that: moments. When people weren't there, she could get quite down and frustrated. Her moods could swing quite violently. She was struggling with the pain caused by the fragments still in her spine, and struggling with how to communicate how she felt about that as well. She could lash out verbally, become angry out of nothing, and I'd have to check myself and remind myself of what it was really about.

I got into a routine of making her a cup of tea before I went to school. I'd get ready for school, ask her if she wanted one, make it and leave it on the table for her before I headed out. One morning, I knocked on her door as usual, to ask if she'd like a cup of tea.

Why the fuck do you have to ask me every day if I want a fucking cup of tea? she shouted at me. Why can't you just fucking make it?

I paused. I nearly said, I'm asking because it's polite, but I checked myself and made the cup of tea instead. *This isn't about me,* I thought to myself. *Maybe she's had a bad night. Maybe she's in pain. Maybe me asking her has hit a different type of nerve: that somehow it's reinforced the point that she isn't as independent as before.* I don't know. I didn't ask her. And I didn't ask her after that day if she wanted a cup of tea. I just made it and put it on the table for her before I left for school.

Thirteen

The trial of Inspector Lovelock took place in January 1987. It was not long after Mum had returned from Stoke Mandeville. The joy of having her back quickly gave way to thoughts about whether justice would be served.

To my twelve-and-a-half-year-old self, the case was self-evident. That was true for most people in Brixton as well. A poll for the *Voice* newspaper in the month after the shooting found that 95 per cent of the Black community thought that Lovelock should be charged with attempted murder. But the charge that the Crown Prosecution Service had opted for was unlawful and malicious wounding. I was too young to understand what that meant and why the charge wasn't attempted murder. But I knew what I had witnessed and what the outcome should be.

The trial took place at the Old Bailey in central London. I was called as a witness. It was a short but surreal experience. The Old Bailey felt huge, cold and intimidating. It was like walking into one of those courtroom dramas you see on TV but with the cold, hard sting that this was really happening. I was nervous and glad that all I had to do was point out who Lovelock was. That was easy. I was never going to forget his face in a hurry. I did the identification and then I was free to go. I was glad to get out of there.

Apart from that, I didn't really get involved in the trial. As a witness, I don't think I could have gone to watch, even if I had wanted to. My mum went to court every day, though I think she must have sat in a nearby room and waited for news. She was represented by Paul Boateng, then a barrister, who had previously worked on the Scrap Sus Campaign. In 2002, by then a Labour politician, he became the UK's first Black cabinet minister, as Chief Secretary to the Treasury in Tony Blair's administration.

Lovelock's defence was that the whole thing was some sort of terrible mistake. In his opening statement, he said: My reaction was totally reflex and a total accident caused by my tensing whilst having my finger on the trigger. I certainly had no intention whatsoever of firing my gun ... I always knew I could never fire unless fired at first. This was a terrible accident which I will always regret.

Once the prosecution and defence had completed their cases, the presiding judge, Mr Justice Leonard, had some words of advice for the jury in his summing up. He told them to put aside any sympathy they had for my mum in reaching their decision: It would be quite astonishing if you did not [feel sympathy]. She has suffered appalling injury. You saw her and you know what he has done to her. And you may have drawn the conclusion that she is a perfectly nice lady. But sympathy for Mrs Groce is not a basis for your decision. In particular you must not feel that because of the terrible injury suffered by Mrs Groce, someone ought to be held responsible.

On Lovelock, the judge reminded the jury of his reputation for integrity and reliability: You should bear the fact that he has a good character in mind when you consider whether he has spoken the truth or not.

The jury retired. After four hours of deliberation, they came back with a verdict. Lovelock was not guilty of the charges against him!

Speaking on behalf of the family, Paul Boateng said: The fact that my client received a life-shattering blow at the hands of Inspector Lovelock remains unaltered by this verdict. She will have to live with the consequences for the rest of her life, just as the officer will have to live with the knowledge of what he has done for the rest of his. Nothing can ever really compensate her for what has happened. She meanwhile continues to pick up the pieces of her life as best she can without bitterness or hatred and wishes only to be left alone to do so.

When the verdict came through, I was shocked. Angry. Furious. I couldn't believe it. But my mum wasn't. It was almost as though she was expecting it.

Lee, she shrugged. The police are a force. You can't fight the force. And that's it.

It was difficult to get my head round what the jury had decided. It felt wrong. It felt unfair. But that was how things were.

Lovelock, who had been suspended on full pay since the shooting, returned to active duty. He faced no disciplinary proceedings at the Met.

Fourteen

The years that followed the court case were a continuous struggle, with money being an ongoing issue. My mum went through solicitor after solicitor trying to resolve the compensation situation. I was too young to be involved, except to see them come for the discussions and then to be replaced by somebody else. I could see the frustrations and the toll the process was taking on my mum. Eventually, she found a solicitor by thumbing through the Yellow Pages and picking a number at random. It turned out that the solicitor she'd chosen, Stephen Burton, was disabled and in a wheelchair as well: that helped in building trust with him, and he stayed to represent her for the rest of the process.

That process was a long one. Compensation didn't come until 1993, eight years after my mum was left paralysed. Eight years!

Those eight years were essentially my teenage ones, and the fact that Mum wasn't working and we were waiting for this mythical cheque to arrive meant that money was continually tight. We lived off a mixture of benefits, community support and the occasional advance offset against the compensation. I felt awkward, asking her for money for things like school dinners. I would rather go hungry. When she did give me money, my immediate instinct was to save it, in case I needed it later. Hand to mouth was how we somehow made it through.

One summer, my trainers began to fall apart. I didn't want to tell Mum because I knew how much pressure she was under for money. I took the bus up to the West End and went into a shoe shop, everything white and shiny: the floors, the walls, the ledges that the shoes sat on. My heartbeat was in my throat.

They always put the right trainer on display and it's normally my size. I took one down from the shelf and asked a shop assistant to get me the pair. He dutifully went into the storeroom and came back with the other one in a shoebox. I tried it on.

No thanks, I said.

He shrugged and was only half watching me. I put the right one that had been on display back in the shoebox and kept the left one; I said I'd put it back on the shelf. Instead, I walked out with it and headed into the next shop down the road. I spotted the trainer I needed, the right shoe to make up a pair with the left one I'd already stolen. Adrenalin racing, I took it down, slipped it into my bag next to the other trainer and walked towards the exit.

Just before I got to the door, a security guard grabbed my arm and told me to follow him up to the office. He was a big guy and his grip was firm; there was no way I was going to be able to wriggle free and make a run for it. If my heart had been going fast before, now it was pumping nineteen to the dozen. The security guard asked me to open my bag and take out the contents. I pulled out the brand-new pair of trainers.

I'm sorry, I said, looking down at the floor. I felt like I might cry. What would Mum say if she found out?

The security guard sat down opposite me. What do you think you're doing? he asked. Why did you think you could just take them?

I don't know, I said. It's, well, my mum can't afford to buy me any new ones. So I was just trying to get some myself. So she wouldn't have to worry.

The security guard looked down at my feet, and the faded pair of trainers I was wearing. Then he nodded towards the phone on the desk. He said, I'm meant to call the police at this point, you know that? They'll arrest you, take you down the station, charge you. It's a slam-dunk case.

But instead, he pushed the phone away from himself. He said, I don't think I'm going to do that, not today. He looked at me again. I suspected that, in his position, he heard all sorts of sob stories. But he seemed to know that my one was genuine. He nodded towards the door.

He said, Go on. Get out of here before I change my mind.

Fifteen

When I'd first returned to school after the shooting, I'd found the readjustment difficult. On one of my first days back, this kid, Arnie, came up to me. Arnie wasn't his real name, but we called him that after the character Arnold in the TV show *Diff'rent Strokes*.

Lee, he'd shouted, in front of everyone. They rioted for your mum. Everyone rioted for your mum!

I hated everyone looking at me and I wished the floor would open up and swallow me. I hated the notoriety. If I was a different sort of person, maybe I'd have played up to it, but every time someone brought it up I shut the topic down.

But while I didn't make a deal of it with the other kids, what I did clock pretty quickly was that the teachers treated me a bit differently. If I messed up or messed around, they weren't as harsh on me as with the other kids. I remember talking back to a teacher one time. That would be an automatic detention. But the teacher just told me off and continued the lesson. Wow, I thought. Maybe this wasn't so all bad after all.

One teacher went further, a guy called Mr Rush. When I did behave badly enough to be kicked out of lessons, I'd be sent to see him. Those excluded were sat with Mr Rush until they were allowed back into class again. But Mr Rush wasn't a disciplinarian-type teacher. He was softly spoken, a gentle and thoughtful soul. I found that I didn't mind being sent out of lessons if it meant I could sit and talk to him. He was the one teacher who was genuinely interested in who I was. Mr Rush was also the only teacher ever to come and visit my mum at home. Going to school for a parents' evening would have been a huge undertaking, so Mr Rush went to see her instead. I really appreciated that.

As well as finding a teacher who had my back, I also found that with a group of friends. When I started secondary school, I was put in a class with a kid called Damien. He'd also been at my primary school and was a real wind-up merchant. He'd always be nudging me, putting things on my head, anything to get a reaction. More often than not, we'd start play fighting, and quickly escalate to fighting for real. The teachers got bored of separating us and put us in different classes. As it turned out, that was the best thing that could have happened to me. In my new class, I found a friend-ship group that I am still in touch with today. Wayne, Martin and Steven, who ended up being the best man at my wedding. However tough times got, and they continued to get tough, at least I faced them in the knowledge that I had some support.

Back home, it was a continual battle to stop Mum declining further. Because she'd stopped going out and wasn't moving enough, she began to get bedsores, and then because the bedsores were painful, that stopped her from moving still further. The NHS paid for a special bed which gave her extra support and she had to stay in that until the bedsores had healed. At one point, she had to go back into Stoke Mandeville and have another operation. They took a part of a bone out, again to try and alleviate things, and that was followed by a further period of rehabilitation.

One time, around 1991, she sat on a pen lid but because she

couldn't feel down there, it got embedded in her leg and created another sore. As that developed, the body rejected the treatment the doctors had given her. The sore became an infection, right down into her bone. It got to the point where they were talking about amputating the leg to deal with it. That took my mum right down mentally. She really didn't want to do that. I sat next to her in her hospital bed in King's and she was adamant.

I'd rather die, she said. My legs don't work, but I'd rather die with them than live without them.

As she lay there, she listened to one song on a loop. It was an eighties gospel song by the singer Tramaine Hawkins, called 'What Shall I Do?' In the song, the singer is asking God directly for advice and help. I remember so clearly her listening to that song, the choir coming in halfway through echoing off the white hospital walls, prickling goosebumps up the back of my neck, as she sat propped up in bed in her regulation hospital gown, tears streaming down her face. I felt helpless watching her – just so sad that she'd ended up in this position, and that the only place she had left was to turn to the Lord and ask him. Whether it was him answering her plea I don't know, but the doctors went on to find a way to deal with the infection and save her leg.

After

Sixteen

Change.org, the site which had hosted the petition, gave me advice on what to do next: ceremonially hand over the signatures at 10 Downing Street. Brixton is only three miles as the crow flies from Whitehall, but it might as well be a different world.

I contacted Chuka Umunna, our local MP, to see if he could help. At the time, he was relatively new to parliament, and he was beginning to make a few waves. He was a natural with the media and was appearing on TV programmes like *Question Time* a lot. This was when Barack Obama was president of the United States, and it felt to me as though there was a bit of a young Obama vibe to him. He was one of those people who was talked up as a future party leader and he was clearly ambitious.

When I first contacted him, he wasn't as responsive to our cause as I'd hoped he would be. It took a while before we had a sit-down meeting with him. The first time Lisa and I went to meet him was at a community centre in Tulse Hill. When we chatted, I got the sense that he was trying to manage my expectations as to what we might achieve. I remember him asking, What's your end goal? and whether my aim was to get the police to recognise the trauma they'd caused and get them to pay damages. Did I really want to create a situation where I was publicly exposing and calling the police out, and was I prepared for the fallout that might come from that?

I explained that none of this was my concern at this point: all I wanted was a fair inquest, to allow the truth to be heard, and to get proper recognition for what had happened to my mum.

I imagine lots of people approach the situation the wrong way round when it comes to their local MPs. Because there are often so many people asking for help, when they get it or even ask for it, it's in an 'it would be an honour if you could support us' way. But it shouldn't be like that. I was his constituent, he was representing me – that was the honour, not the other way around.

There's a scene from the movie *Seven*, where John Doe, played by the actor Kevin Spacey, says, Wanting people to listen, you can't just tap them on the shoulder any more. You have to hit them with a sledgehammer, and then you'll notice you've got their strict attention.

I talked to Chuka straight. I said: You need to be able to look yourself in the mirror and ask yourself, Did I do everything that I could within my power to support this family? If you can answer that question and say that you have, then that's fine. But if you can't, then you're going to have to live with the consequences.

Chuka looked taken aback by that. I can only do what I can do, he replied.

But he stepped up. On the day we went to Downing Street to hand over the petition, he did an interview on the radio, LBC I think, where he explained about what my family and I were doing.

That was a really good interview, I told him afterwards. I liked the way you got our case across.

Thank you, he replied. I've been wondering if you've been happy with what I've been doing. That's important for me to know.

I was. I patted him on the back, and then we hugged. It was a moment – another small but symbolic step of people taking us seriously.

It was strange being outside of 10 Downing Street. Familiar but foreign. As often with things on TV, it turned out to be smaller in real life. The presentation of petitions is symbolic: you have an allotted time slot, you walk up once the press are in position, the box containing the petition is actually empty (the signatures arrive with the government electronically), a man waits behind the door so when you knock on it, it opens straight away, and you have to do it three times to make sure the press have all the pictures they need. But there is power behind ceremony. If I had told my mum when I was eleven that one day I would be knocking on the Prime Minister's door for her, she'd never have believed me.

I asked Chuka what he thought our chances were. He was confident that our request was going to be taken seriously, that it would be properly considered. We'd got it in front of the right people, and they would have the right conversations about it. But he was also cautious; we had to wait and see. I left that day in hope rather than expectation that the decision about legal aid would be overturned. We'd seen so many false dawns over the years that until something happened, I wasn't going to believe it.

Then, it was time to wait. The decision took about a week to come through. It rested with the Minister for Justice, who was Chris Grayling. Years later, I saw him at a conference I was at, but I didn't get a chance to speak to him. I would have liked to have done, because I was thankful that the right decision was reached and our legal aid was granted. I would have liked to have had a conversation with him to get a sense of how and why he made that decision. I would have liked to have found out whether he made the decision, or whether it was a civil servant and he'd just signed off on the recommendation. Whoever it was that decided, I was thankful that the right decision had been made..

*

After I set up the petition, a charity called Inquest, which specialises in helping the families of loved ones who've experienced state-related deaths, got in touch and asked if they could help. They found us a solicitor, a guy by the name of Raju Bhatt. He was one of the founders of a firm called Bhatt Murphy, which had been set up in the late 1990s by lawyers passionate about defending civil liberties. I met him in their offices in Shoreditch, east London. When I arrived, it was about five in the evening, but despite it being the end of the day, the place was still buzzing and full of energy. The first meeting was a bit awkward. I was explaining what the situation was, when Raju found out he had a family emergency and was going to have to leave. I continued with one of the other lawyers, but wasn't sure what the outcome would be. I left wondering if this was another false start.

The second meeting was much more successful. This time I had Raju's full attention. He said the firm wanted to represent me, whether or not we secured legal aid. The feeling of relief was huge. I breathed out as if I'd been holding my breath for the many months since the process began. When the meeting was over, I got out of their offices and immediately started calling my sisters, telling them the good news. I would never have stopped trying to get legal aid, though. We deserved it. The rest of the lawyers involved were all provided by the police, and therefore by the state; the family of the bereaved should have been entitled to it too.

Once legal aid was confirmed, suddenly all the lawyers and barristers who'd helped us earlier got back in touch. Now there was money on the table, they were interested in getting involved again. One of them went on social media to say, 'I'm glad we were able to secure legal aid.' *We?* I thought. One person started talking about how we might receive compensation from the Met, and to remember them and possible foundations I could donate it to. I don't begrudge anyone trying to make a living, and I was hugely appreciative of all the time these various people had given to help us.

But I felt that we now had a firm in our corner who were about the cause not the cash, and that was who we were going to stick with.

The inquest was set for 30 June 2014. We had two and a half months to prepare. I was scared but I felt confident too. When I'd started the process, I hadn't realised what lay ahead was a mountain. Now I was halfway up it and I couldn't believe how many people I'd managed to bring with me – including all of my family, who were now firmly involved and had started believing we could do it, too. The hardest part lay ahead – but look how far we'd come.

Before

Seventeen

At 10.30 p.m. on Thursday 22 April 1993, a young man and his friend were on West Hall Road in Eltham, looking for a bus to take them home. The young man had spent the day at Blackheath Bluecoat School, where he was studying technology and physics, then he'd gone shopping in Lewisham before going to his uncle's house, where he'd met up with his friend and played video games. They'd originally got on a direct bus home to Plumstead, but having realised its route would take them a while they got off to catch a quicker bus. The pair separated: the young man walked down to the junction with Dickson Road, to see if he could see a bus coming. His friend was waiting further down the road when he saw a group of six white youths approaching on the other side of the road.

The friend called out to see if the young man had spotted a bus coming.

'What, what, nigger?' one of the youths shouted at the young man. The six surrounded him. 'Engulfed' was the word used to describe the incident afterwards. The young man was stabbed twice, five inches deep, in his front. One wound partially collapsed his right lung. It was probably only because of his unusual fitness – the young man competed for his local athletics club – that he was able to run afterwards. As the group of youths dispersed down Dickson Road, the young man ran in the direction of his friend, towards Shooters Hill. His friend ran towards him for about a hundred metres, before the young man collapsed. He was wearing several layers of clothing, which meant that there was no particular trail of blood as he ran. But he was bleeding heavily and he either died when he fell, or soon after. By the time an ambulance arrived, it was too late.

Today, the spot where the young man died is marked by a simple, unobtrusive granite plaque. It's nestled under the shade of a tree, and in the autumn is marked by a scattering of leaves. Flowers are sometimes left there, particularly on the anniversary. But it's also been attacked over the years – it's been chipped at, spat at, had paint and flammable liquids poured on it, glass smashed over it. But the plaque remains, its wording quiet, powerful, undimmed:

In memory of
Stephen Lawrence.
13.9.1974
22.4.1993
May He Rest in Peace.

The murder of Stephen Lawrence was one of those events of such magnitude that I remember exactly where I was when I heard the news. I was at a friend's house, Martin's, aka Speng, in Kennington. A whole group of us were there. It must have been the Friday, the day after the murder. My immediate thought was that we should respond.

That's an attack on all of us, I said. That boy who has been killed, that could easily have been any one of us.

That was part of the reason that Stephen's death hit so hard. He was similar in age to me; he'd grown up in south London, just as

104

I had. The events leading up to the stabbing were so everyday, so ordinary, the attack seemed unfathomable. There was a real 'there but for the grace of God' feel to what happened.

We should go, I told my friends. We should go to Eltham right now, to show that we're not going to stand for this shit any longer.

Are you sure? one of my friends said. I mean, what are we going to achieve by going there? And what are we going to find when we turn up there? What are we going to be confronted with?

We sat and we argued. I was all for going but the others were split. To be fair, I didn't really know what we would do once we got there. I wasn't thinking that clearly. But although I ended up being talked out of it, my anger remained undimmed. What had happened to Stephen Lawrence couldn't go unchecked, because the next time a group of white youths confronted a Black boy on his own, it could be any of us.

The threat from being attacked by a gang in this way, by white youths, by racists, was one that had been instilled in me from a young age. I was about eight or nine when I first became aware that I could be beaten up simply for being Black. I was told to be aware of gangs of youths and not to be out by myself late at night. And if I should ever see a group, particularly of skinheads, then I was to run for it.

The driving force behind this threat was the National Front. In the 1977 elections for the Greater London Council, the National Front finished fourth, winning 5.3 per cent of the vote. Their strength in south London was reinforced by the organisation's headquarters being in Croydon, and marches being held in places like Lewisham – neither of which were a million miles away from where we lived.

In the early 1980s, as mentioned earlier, the National Front had a policy of recruiting skinheads and football hooligans to their cause. This continued under a succession of leaders, with an attempt to build up a core group of activists, with a particular drive among skinhead subculture. That was the backdrop we grew up against. And if legitimised isn't quite the right word, the sort of atmosphere it created set the tone for how many people behaved. People weren't concerned about holding such opinions publicly.

Just down the road, at private school Dulwich College, a teenage Nigel Farage was being educated. In 1981, one of the teachers wrote to the headmaster, asking him not to make Farage a prefect because of his 'publicly professed racist and neo-fascist views'. In 2016, in an open letter to Farage in the *Independent*, a former peer of Farage's wrote: I vividly recall the keen interest you had in two initials of your name written together as a signature and the bigoted symbol that represents.

Farage said that any claim he was involved with far-right politics was 'utterly untrue', though did say, Of course I said some ridiculous things, not necessarily racist things. It depends how you define it.

What Farage himself did or didn't believe as a teenager isn't really the point. It's more that from nearby private schools downwards, a flirtation and interest in such views was something if not considered acceptable, then at the least accepted. And what that meant on the street was, if you weren't careful, and didn't keep an eye out, trouble was always potentially around the corner. Growing up, there were areas you just didn't go as a Black kid. Bermondsey was one. Parts of Croydon were known for being iffy. And Eltham, where Stephen Lawrence was murdered, was another place with a reputation for being racist. I was aware that once you went beyond your regular haunts, beyond Brixton, Clapham, Peckham, then you could be at risk. Anywhere you suddenly noticed how few Black people were around, that was when you should start to get worried. But you didn't even have to travel that far to experience a racist attack. Sometimes it started on your own doorstep.

*

A few years before the murder of Stephen Lawrence, after we'd moved out of Normandy Road and into Gipsy Hill, there was a teenage white boy on our estate called Stephen. Stephen, his brother and his dad, they didn't like us – me and my Black friends. It seemed as if, whenever I walked past, they'd be there, standing in the doorway of their house, arms folded, staring at me. Nothing was ever said, but that eyeballing was meant to intimidate. It felt as though it had a racist undertone, the disdain and disgust they would look at me with. Going past their house felt like running the gauntlet.

One day, I was on my way to school, waiting for the bus to come. As the bus pulled up, Stephen was there, about to get off. He got off the bus, saw me, gave me the look. Then, out of nowhere, he hit me with a sucker punch. It was completely unprovoked; I hadn't said anything to him at all. I tried to come back at him, but we were quickly pulled apart by other people who were waiting at the stop. He was shoved off on his way, and I got on the bus, my eye throbbing.

By the time I got to school, people were staring at me. I went to the toilets; the image of myself in the mirror was horrible. My eye was red and bloodshot, the skin around all raised and swollen. My friends asked me what had happened.

Hang on, one of them said. You got attacked by a white boy? For nothing?

The way they responded, I felt embarrassed at what happened.

You can't let that lie, another friend said. You need to confront him.

As we carried on talking, I got increasingly worked up, like the coil of a spring being tightened. They were right; I couldn't just let him get away with what he'd done, thinking he could attack a Black boy without comeback. I'd been attacked because of the colour of my skin. Was I just going to accept that, or was I going to respond?

Together with a couple of my friends, I went over to his school one lunchtime. Bold as brass. We walked into their playground, real lion's den stuff. I stopped someone and asked where Stephen was. They pointed him out to me. I walked straight over and beat him up. I'm not a fighter, but I was so worked up, I tore at him, to the point that he couldn't take any more. He was screaming for help. A small crowd had gathered around me and my friends to see what was going on. Then we ran off, headed back to our own school and continued the day as though nothing had happened.

The whole thing was like a silent movie. Both in the original eyeballing, and in both the fights, not a single word was spoken. In a way, that just emphasised what the whole episode had been about. It was a straight colour thing, nothing else to it. Stephen and his family moved away from the estate quite soon after the incident. I'm not sure I ever saw him again.

That incident gave me confidence. It gave me belief that, when confronted with that sort of incident, I could and should respond. And the next time it happened, that's exactly what I did. This time the incident took place at my own school and the timing couldn't have been worse: it was just before I started sitting my GCSEs.

My secondary school was multicultural. I don't really know what the exact breakdown was; I'd guess that it was about 50 per cent Black, although that may be me misremembering, on account of who I was hanging out with. But a good percentage of the students were Black and there was also quite a sizeable community of Chinese heritage too. We didn't mix that much, but we respected each other. I remember one time my friends and I were playing football with a can, kicking it around. I whacked it and it flew up and hit this Chinese boy, who was a couple of years older than me, in the nuts. He walked up to me and kicked me in the face – a Bruce Lee-style karate kick. That hurt – my nose was bleeding – but at the end of school he came and found me and apologised. No hard feelings, except for my nose.

Because of the balance in the school, racism was never really an issue: you didn't hear racist terms of abuse. But then, just before I was sitting my GCSEs, it got around that this white boy called Tony had called one of the Black boys a monkey. By then, I was one of the older boys, who was respected and looked up to in the school, and I felt a responsibility to take a stand. After school, a group of about half a dozen waited for him. We told him what we thought of him, and roughed him up. Nothing too heavy, but enough that he'd get the message about what would happen if he said anything racist again.

I knew what might happen as a result of this and sure enough, I got suspended. In terms of my education and what I was going to do next, getting involved might not have been the smartest thing to do. But it felt the right thing to do. I had to argue with them to let me back in to take my exams, with the help of Mr Rush. Otherwise I would have left school with zero qualifications. Eventually, they said I could, but they didn't relent on the suspension. It felt harsh – the school was much more interested in what we'd done than what had been said to trigger it. Which kind of reinforced why we'd done it. We were the only ones who took the racism seriously, and the only ones prepared to do anything about it. I don't agree with intimidation as a form of justice, but that was the stark reality. In the absence of justice, it was all we had.

Eighteen

In year six of primary school, I had a teacher who I will call Mr Bright. He was tall, domineering and a bully. At the end of each lesson he made us sing a song that went 'We don't want no education, we don't want to go to school, let the teacher take the blame. Oh what a blinking shame!'

One day, with summer outside the window, the whole of my class was in detention – Mr Bright loved handing out detentions. We sat in our chairs waiting for the fifteen minutes of enforced silence to end. Someone's chair scraped the floor; Mr Bright reset the clock. Someone sniffed; Mr Bright reset the clock. Someone tutted, annoyed; Mr Bright reset the clock. On and on until *finally* he let us go. We ran out the classroom, and some of my friends and I moaned about him to each other, saying things like Mr Bright is an f'ing bastard, and not bothering to keep our voices down because we were angry. Mr Bright came after us. He ran down the stairs and jumped over the banister to block us leaving. He lined four of us up against the wall. You think this is funny? he asked, taking turns to conk us, bam, on the head. He grabbed our hair, twisted it until we were crying.

One of my friends, Jason Collins (RIP), said to him, I'm going to get my dad.

Mr Bright picked him up and slammed him against the wall. Get your dad, he said, like he didn't give a shit.

This was my formative experience with authority. A few months later, the police broke into my house and shot my mum.

My first encounter with the police as a teenager was when I was fourteen. Ever since the shooting, my attitude towards the police had changed. How could it not? I no longer wanted to be a policeman. I knew them now for what they were, like we all did. They weren't protection, they were trouble.

It was a quiet, calm, early autumn evening, and I was walking home after hanging out with some friends. I heard this phut-phut sound of an engine behind me and saw one of my friends, a guy called Julian, lurching down the street on a moped. He wasn't driving it well, jumping it forwards and back as he revved and braked. He pulled up alongside me.

Hey, where'd you get that? I asked.

My friend just grinned: You want a ride or what?

I climbed on the back and held tight (I'd seen how he'd been driving the thing).

You ready? my friend asked, revving the engine. Then, with a shout, we were shooting down the road. Whoa! The buildings down the side zipped past in a blur. I could feel the pull of the speed, the chill of the breeze as we blasted down under the streetlights. God knows where my friend had got the bike from. Probably best not to know and just enjoy it, I thought.

We rode on down into Brixton. The streets were busier there, a few people glancing up as we spun down the road. I was caught between grinning from the experience and hiding back in case anyone saw us. Though with the way my friend was revving the engine and tooting the tinny horn, we were difficult to miss.

We rode on to where the 28s were hanging out: Corners, an

amusement arcade on Brixton Water Lane. The 28s were a local gang. I wasn't a full member, though I had friends who were. I was more of an affiliate. At the time, there was a rivalry between the 28s and another local gang, the Untouchables. Even if you weren't a member, you picked your side. The 28s was mine.

Corners was our territory, a place where all the members of the gang would gather, somewhere you knew you could go to be safe. As we drove up, my friend gave a little sharp stop, just to try and impress everyone. We were probably the youngest kids there – most of the other 28s were that bit older – so there was an element of us trying to fit in, to show that we were worthy. My friend jumped off and one of the other members climbed onto the moped, with me still on the back. Before I could get off, we were going for another spin. I was a bit more nervous this time – the guy driving was more senior, and he put the moped through its paces.

I can't remember if it was the flash of blue light I saw or the whirr of the siren I heard first, but as if out of nowhere police vans appeared. With a lurching feeling, shit, I realised that it was us they were after. The guy who was driving swung the moped around; I was clinging on to try to stop myself from falling off, digging my fingers into his back. I wasn't sure what he was going to do, whether he was going to try outrunning them, to slip through a gap and head off into the night. As we spun round, I wasn't sure that he was quite certain what to do. And then the moment was over, the vans were blocking the road and the police poured out towards us.

As the moped pulled to a stop, I was grabbed off the back by a police officer. It was a rough shove, a yank, torn backwards by a fistful of my top. Then I was shoved towards the van. The gang member who had been riding the bike, he was being pushed there too, but he pushed back a bit more. His hands were up, not in surrender, but more of a 'hey, don't touch me' sort of way. It was all happening so fast and it was so new to me, I didn't know what

112

I should do but I blindly stumbled and followed. Our arms were bent behind our backs and handcuffs were put on very tightly. So tightly that my wrists were still bruised days later.

As we got to the van, the door was swung open. There was a police officer there, indicating with his thumb for us to get inside. Come on then, monkeys, he said. In you get.

I was so surprised that it took me a second to register what he said. But then, just in case I was mistaken, the police officer repeated it.

You heard what I said, monkey. In you go.

My reaction was almost to giggle. It was so horrific and ridiculous at the same time, it was all I could do to stop myself from laughing. I climbed into the back of the van, with a helping shove from the police officer. The older gang member followed me in with an All right, I'm going! as the police officer tried to shove him in as well. As the door slammed shut behind us, we sat down in the dark on two hard benches. There was a grille window between us and the front seats and the police officer who had just shut us in climbed into his seat and looked back at us. That's enough from you fucking monkeys now, all right? he said. There was laughter from the other officers in the front.

By this point, my surprise at what we were being called was starting to be replaced by something else. Anger. I looked over to the older guy who was in there with me. It was dark in the back and so it was hard to see his expression, but it hit me that he wasn't responding to the language. It was nothing new to him, I realised. He'd been arrested before, he'd heard such words so often that either it just washed over him, or he'd learned not to react, not to give them the satisfaction of letting it rile him. I'm not sure what was more shocking – the police officer saying what he said, or this guy ground down to the point of not responding. The normalisation of racist language to the point of nobody blinking, on either side. It was a sobering moment.

At the police station, they put us in separate cells. I didn't have any idea what the rules were – I was fourteen, could they do that? But I was smart enough not to start questioning it. The cell was small and bare, and I sat on a wooden bench, swinging my legs and wondering what was going to happen next. I wasn't scared, not really, though I think that was as much naivety as anything else. If I knew more of the stories of what happened to Black men in those cells, then I would have been a lot more fearful.

I don't remember how long I was in the cell for, but eventually I was hauled into the interview room, where I was grilled about the moped. The police officer doing the interview fired all sorts of questions at me, but I dead-batted them back. I wasn't going to grass my friend up, or say anything that would incriminate me or him or anyone else.

The officer continued: Where's the moped from? Who stole it? Do you know what the punishment for stealing a bike is? Not to mention driving without a licence, underage, without a helmet, attempting to resist arrest?

He reeled off a long list of possible charges, trying to intimidate me. But I held firm.

Eventually, I just wanted the stalemate to end. I said: I didn't know the bike was stolen. I assumed it was his. I just got on the back of it for a ride.

As I was taken back down to the cells, my main concern was not the police, but what my mum would say when she found out. Because of my age, they needed to get someone to come and get me out of there, which meant they were going to ring home. I felt really bad, that I'd let her down. The thought that the police might turn up at her door because of what I'd done – I didn't like that at all.

I sat back down on the bench, adrenalin pumping, and thought, *So this is what it's like.* I was pleased with myself for getting through the interview, for keeping my head up. I thought it would be useful experience for if it happened again; I'd know what to do next time. I felt like I'd cemented my place in the gang, too – that I'd shown I could be trusted, could take it just as much as the older members. On the street, I knew that would stand me in good stead. My credibility had just gone up a notch.

Eventually, the cell door opened and I was escorted out, cautioned and told, Someone's come to pick you up.

It was my dad waiting for me out front. He had this look of disappointment on his face, but he didn't really say anything. At the time, I didn't know he'd once been in trouble himself, but maybe he was remembering that, thinking some circle-of-life stuff about seeing his son in the same situation. But my dad wasn't one for talking about that sort of stuff, so who knows? We didn't really speak. When we got out the front of the station we went our separate ways: I walked back to my house and he went back to wherever he was staying.

When I got home, Mum gave me a right telling off. It was her who had called my dad to pick me up. She was cussing away, about how stupid I'd been: Do you want to get yourself locked up? You could have got yourself killed!

The anger and shouting I could deal with. But the look of disappointment on her face floored me. I didn't want to see that again.

Nineteen

But, being young and Black and getting arrested was part and parcel of growing up in Brixton. I was far from a bad kid – anything but, in most respects – and yet it was still quite hard not to get arrested. I reckon in total I was arrested somewhere between ten and fifteen times over that period: each and every time it was over nothing; each and every time I was released without charge.

It didn't take much for a situation to blow up. However straight and polite you might be, there was always that chance that things might go off, the hostility getting ramped up and, out of nowhere, it was all 'you're coming with me' and 'maybe you'll be more helpful down the station'. Sometimes it felt like it came out of fear on their side, a nervousness they masked by acting tough.

One incident I remember getting arrested for was being on a bus and getting into an altercation with the driver. The driver stopped the bus and wouldn't drive on until I'd got off. I was with a friend and didn't like being made to look a fool in front of him and everyone else, who were now turning to look at me. So I stood, or rather sat, my ground. The driver called the police, who turned up in a completely unnecessary squeal of lights and sirens. Rather than attempting to defuse the situation, they came on board all heavy handed. And then I was arrested, and back in those cells again.

I knew the deal by now. I sat there, waiting it out, either to be interviewed or released or bailed. But this time, while I was waiting, the small metal hatch on the cell door opened. I looked over from the bench I was sitting on, and there was a white police officer just stood there observing me.

Lee Lawrence, he said with a kind of smirk on his face. You're Cherry Groce's son.

At the mention of my mum, I jolted. I stood up and walked over towards the door.

That's right, I said.

The man sneered and said: It's a pity she didn't die.

Before I could respond, he slammed the flap shut. I could hear his footsteps echoing off down the corridor, and what sounded like a laugh.

In some respects, it was good that I was stuck in that cell, because I was absolutely steaming. I was bouncing off the walls with anger. After everything our family had been through, everything as a result of police action, here was a police officer, taunting me about what happened. It's difficult to put into words just how upsetting those comments were. It was like putting salt into the wound. Even now, all these years later, I can still feel myself getting riled up just thinking about it.

I got bailed on that occasion. When I was allowed out of the cell, I looked around for the police officer who'd taunted me, but he had gone – must have been off shift. I had to go back to the station with a solicitor, to be interviewed under caution. But my anger over what the police officer had said to me hadn't died down. If anything, it was hardening and getting stronger. I was wound up to the point that I wanted to be ready to confront the guy. That if I saw him again, I'd be able to respond. I was ready to take the

117

consequences. I genuinely felt that I was prepared to go to prison if he repeated what he'd said about my mum.

On the day of the interview, I bought a screwdriver. Thinking about it now, it was an absolutely crazy thing to do, but on the day of the interview I had it slipped up my sleeve, ready for me to use if I needed it. I didn't tell my solicitor about any of this, but as we walked into the police station together I could feel my heart pumping away about it. Heading into a police station with a concealed weapon? I know. But that's how strongly I felt.

The solicitor and I were shown into the interview room. As we sat there, waiting, I could feel the cold of the metal up against my skin. Then the door opened, and it was the same guy. The police officer who'd made those comments about my mum was the one who was down to interview me.

I couldn't let it go.

Say what you said about my mum again, I said.

The police officer, who had been fiddling with the tape, stopped and looked at me.

I'm sorry, what are you talking about?

You know exactly what I'm talking about, I replied. When I was in the cell and you came up to me. What was that you said through the door about my mum, again?

I was eyeballing him now. I could sense my solicitor leaning forward and looking at me, but I wasn't taking my gaze off the police officer.

I'm sorry, I don't know what you're talking about, the officer said, breaking my gaze and glancing at my solicitor and then back at me again. This is the first time that we've spoken.

It was one of those moments when you can feel the tension in the room. One of those moments where your life could turn in an instant.

Is it OK if we start the interview now? the police officer said.

You're not going to repeat what you said?

Mr Lawrence, I'm afraid I really don't know what you're talking about.

The police officer looked down at his notes. At that moment, I recognised him for the coward he was: he was quite happy to make comments behind the safety of a cell door; he didn't have the guts to say them directly to my face, in front of other people. I sat back, shuffled my sleeve and slid the screwdriver back up my arm.

After

Twenty

Long-lost report. That was the subject of the email that I got with the police report of my mum's shooting attached.

I was upstairs in our loft conversion when it pinged into my inbox. The document was as long as the time I felt I'd waited for it. I printed it out, twice. I gave one to Gem. She sat downstairs, I sat in our box room-cum-home office. Gem had a pink highlighter pen. I had a yellow. We both started to read and mark up.

The report was compiled by John Domaille, who at the time was Assistant Chief Constable of West Yorkshire Police. As was customary in situations such as these, a member of an outside force was brought in to investigate. Domaille had twenty years' experience as an authorised firearms officer: he had been involved in numerous firearms operations and been raid group leader on many of these. Having become too old for such operations, Domaille had then worked as a senior officer authorising such operations. In other words, he was vastly experienced in this area.

The full report is a huge document, hundreds of pages long. In the weeks after the shooting, Domaille investigated what happened that Saturday morning, and in the run-up to the raid, in detail. He interviewed all relevant parties and drew conclusions on a number of potential criminal and disciplinary charges against several officers involved in the operation. Most prominent was Inspector Lovelock, but his investigation also looked at allegations against those involved in the planning. The report finishes with a list of conclusions and recommendations, not just about Lovelock personally, but also about the behaviour of the police more generally.

Maybe because it was prepared internally, for police use, Domaille was more forthright and straightforward in his thoughts than he might have been if it was a public document. There isn't a way to describe how I felt reading it, so I won't try, but what follows is a précis of what we were allowed to include later, at the inquest.

Domaille began by describing the sequence of events, beginning on the lunchtime of Thursday 26 September 1985, when Michael is alleged to have pointed a sawn-off shotgun at officers in Stamford Street. These were officers from Hertfordshire Police, following up an armed robbery in Hertfordshire, who had come in to Metropolitan Police territory. They called the Met for assistance. At the Stamford Street property, they found the weapon in question, but no sign of Michael.

That afternoon, there was a phone conversation between Hertfordshire and the Met, in which the former said Michael was no longer wanted in connection with the robbery. The Met, however, continued to search for him. Strangely, he turned up at Lambeth Magistrates' Court as a visitor later that day, where he provided his name and gave his address as 22 Normandy Road.

On the Friday, after having searched various properties for Michael, the discussion came round to Normandy Road. This was discussed at Kennington CID, and it was decided the property should be visited by armed officers. This was a joint operation between Kennington and Brixton: Superintendent Murray, at Brixton, tasked Chief Inspector Beckett to organise the operation; Lovelock and PC Myerscough were brought over from Kennington as armed officers.

At a Friday lunchtime briefing at Brixton Police Station, Murray told the assembled team that the raid wouldn't take place that afternoon, on the grounds that the house was next door to a busy public house, and also near a children's playground. As Domaille noted: 'What is clear from this briefing is that [there] was a lack of intelligence about the interior of 22 Normandy Road and also the occupancy . . . it was not known whether or how many men, women, children, even dogs would be inside.'

Later that afternoon, a search warrant for Normandy Road was granted. The wording for the search warrant request stated that 'The occupant of this address, 22 Normandy Road, was involved in an incident during which he discharged a sawn-off shotgun whilst police officers were attempting to arrest. He escaped from the premises at which the incident occurred and it is believed that he has returned to the address shown above and is in possession of further firearms.'

Instead, those in the house that Saturday morning were my parents, Juliet, Sharon, Lisa, myself and the two young children of a friend of my mum's. 'Michael Groce does not reside with his other [siblings],' Domaille wrote, 'he is not included in the electoral roll, he is allegedly an infrequent visitor to the house.' At 6 a.m. on the Saturday, a pre-raid briefing was held at Brixton Police Station. The only new information on the house was that Inspector Beckett had seen a light on in a downstairs front window on his way to work. Lovelock was selected as raid group leader.

The armed officers took their positions for the raid. One group at the back of the house saw a light on there – this was my mum, having gone to the kitchen to get a paracetamol to help deal with a toothache – but this was not passed on to Lovelock's team at the front. At 7 a.m. the front door was smashed open with a sledge-hammer. Domaille wrote, 'there is little doubt that this caused a considerable crash since the noise was heard by officers at the rear of the house. There is also little doubt that Inspector Lovelock's tension was at a peak. He describes the blood pounding round his body at that moment and his expectation of confronting an armed and dangerous criminal.'

Lovelock, according to Domaille's report, 'says that he shouted "Armed police!" prior to entering the house'. Domaille notes that one officer in the front groups remembers Lovelock shouting something, but cannot remember what it was; the others there don't recall him shouting anything: 'There is some doubt, therefore, in the mind of the investigating officer that such a warning was in fact given ... none of the house occupants heard such a warning.'

From the hallway, Lovelock kicked open the door to his right. 'The inspector entered the room in what he described as a semi-crouched position with revolver held in both hands pointing in front of him. The inspector denies any intention to fire the weapon, saying it was due to a reflex action when he tensed up and he had not fired consciously. He says his finger must have been on the trigger as he entered the room, but insists the weapon was on double safety.'

Beginning with the planning, Domaille noted that Lambeth Council were not contacted to find out about the property, due to a perceived 'anti-police attitude' and the belief that someone at the council could tip the family off about the raid. He noted, too, that surveillance of Normandy Road was ruled out because of the 'sensitivity of the area' − observation vehicles would quickly be spotted, and the police force lacked Black officers who could carry out more discreet surveillance.

Domaille criticised the size of the raid team as 'inadequate'. Contingencies were not prepared for. Containment, in respect of keeping back members of the public, was patchy. He looked at the possibility of using what he described as a 'direct confrontation technique', such as using a loudhailer or contacting the house in another way, rather than an armed raid. The police operation had ruled this out, but Domaille was less sure: 'if it is realistic that direct confrontation technique was out of the question, then it is firmly believed that the most prudent course of action in this case would have been for the operation not to proceed forthwith, but for an intelligence gathering exercise to take place. To go ahead as planned with a surprise entry with such a lack of information . . . was clearly to take an unnecessary risk . . . the decision made to continue the operation was not reasonable and grave risks were created, both for police and public, which should have been avoided.'

There was criticism, too, of obtaining the original warrant for the raid. Rather than Michael shooting at police while resisting arrest, Domaille concluded that 'the shotgun had been discharged by the suspect during the course of a domestic disagreement in the flat and the visit by the police, a few minutes later, was coincidental'. The information given by the police to obtain the warrant was therefore 'inaccurate', and rather than an immediate urgency to arrest Michael, 'in the circumstances of these events, a warrant was not essential'.

Turning to the Saturday morning itself, Domaille said, 'the raid should not have gone ahead in the manner planned due to the total lack of information'. Of Inspector Lovelock's state of mind, he continued, 'During interview, the inspector denied that the lack of information about the house interior and occupancy contributed to his state of tension. The investigating officer finds this difficult to accept, since there are very clear dangers in carrying out a search over an unknown terrain with the possibility of Groce or any number of people, being anywhere in the house. Inspector Lovelock admits that he had in mind the possibility of male friends of Groce being present.'

Domaille went on to say that, 'Inspector Lovelock was entering a highly dangerous environment with an absence of knowledge about anything or anyone inside. The size of the group was inadequate and it must have exercised his mind about how the remainder of the house was to be secured and how, for example, the unknown friends of Groce were to be dealt with – a number of issues which must have increased his tension. Indeed, this would have been a tense and difficult situation if all the information had been available.'

Rather than facing a group of armed and dangerous criminals, Domaille noted that, 'The inspector was confronted by a West Indian woman, only five foot tall at least two feet away from the muzzle of his outstretched gun moving towards him on reasonable lighting.'

In his conclusions, Domaille criticised again the application of the original warrant as inaccurate, saying of the officer who applied for it that 'his conduct cannot be excused. He had a duty to ensure that the facts that he would provide on oath were accurate.'

He criticised the lack of intelligence-gathering before the raid. 'There would seem no bar to some sort of short-term discreet surveillance, perhaps from a private vehicle to ascertain movement about the house. It is highly probable, for example, that such an observation at school leaving time would reveal the presence of children.'

Domaille said, 'there were clearly serious deficiencies in carrying out the operation as planned. In view of the absence of information it is clear that the raid group were to be placed in considerable danger . . . the most prudent course of action in this case would have been for the operation not to proceed forthwith, but for an intelligence gathering exercise to take place.' He concluded that 'the raid should not have gone ahead in the manner planned, due to the total lack of information . . . the decision to continue the operation was not reasonable and grave risks were created both for public and police, which should have been avoided.'

It's hard to describe what it felt like, reading the original document. It's only a shame that for legal reasons we can't reproduce it in full here. Reading Domaille's unexpurgated, unredacted version was a shocking and emotional experience for me. The detail about the shooting itself brought back painful memories. But what really struck home was all the detail about what happened before the raid. I didn't know anything about that. And the behaviour of the police, and the incompetence of the operation, was just jaw-dropping. More than once, I put my highlighter pen down in disbelief.

I could see why the lawyers didn't want it to be included, even the redacted version. They tried one more time, particularly Lovelock's lawyer, to get it pulled from the inquest. On the Friday before proceedings began the following Monday. Doing it so late in the day felt shady as hell to me. But they didn't win the argument; the coroner agreed for the version above to be included. The truth at last.

Before

Twenty-One

When I was younger, before 28 September 1985 and the spiral of events that happened after it, I'd go to a youth centre after school. It was a ramshackle, run-down building. One of those temporary prefab huts that ended up becoming permanent. There was always plenty to do there: pool, table tennis, lots of creative activities. We'd make stuff out of straws, weave them together to make a basket, that sort of thing. It was popular, lots of people from the Cowley estate would go there.

But the thing that really excited me was the music. At weekends, the people who ran the youth centre set up a sound system, and there'd be a whole party going on. It wasn't a surprise that I liked music so much, given how much my mum loved it and encouraged us to listen to it, but here we listened to stuff that was different to the music my mum liked. Her taste was more soulful and based around the singing and the words, whereas the music that came out of our sound systems had a bit more dub and bass to it. People would then chat lyrics over the top – kind of like rapping, but we called it chatting at the time. One of the groups that owned the precarious stack of speakers that made up the sound system was known as Circuit One. I was desperate to be a part of it, and got myself a role as a box boy. That was the bottom rung of the group – helping carry the speakers around – but it was still cool just to be part of it, to be able to say that you were part of the sound. I found school hard – later I found out I was dyslexic, but at the time the teachers just wrote me off as not trying. Listening to music and being part of Circuit One helped me belong.

Once you'd been a box boy, then you might graduate up to being the DJ: they'd call themselves the selector, choosing the music that was played. There was also the MC, the mic man, who said words over the music. Becoming an MC was what I aspired to be. I never found the courage to get on stage and perform them, but I wrote myself some lyrics, had my introduction all worked out: *My name is Rudy Lee, on the mic MC, I live at 22 Normandy, so let me tell you something about the real Cowley . . .*

Rudy Lee was a persona I'd invented for myself. There were a lot of big personalities in my family. As a young boy, growing up in Brixton among and around strong women, there was a pressure to try and establish yourself. I felt that doubly so, because I had older siblings who were stronger and more resilient than me. But I couldn't step up as me, it just wasn't in my nature. And so that's where the nickname thing came from: standing up as Lee terrified me, but creating this persona, Rudy Lee – that felt like someone who I could grow into and inhabit. There was something appealing about the idea of being a rude boy, the rough-around-the-edges bad boy who was a little bit naughty, a little bit knowing.

Later, when I was a bit older, I took my name from my older brother, Michael, and became Younger Cowboy. And then I became Brandy Lee. That came out of nowhere one evening. Michael was going to the shop and asked us if we wanted anything to drink. I said, Can I get a brandy? Michael said, Lee, you're always drinking brandy. We should call you Brandy Lee.

On my eighteenth birthday my friends and my sisters took me out to a club. My sisters went up to the guy on the mic and asked him if he'd big me up, and say happy birthday.

Big up Brandy Lee, the guy boomed across the room. I don't know who the fuck you are, but happy birthday anyway.

Wow. I remember thinking, *OK, you're going to know who I am one day.* And that was where my musical journey kicked up to the next level. That was when I decided to take it more seriously and make a name for myself. Up to that point, me and my friends had just messed around with the music: everyone did a bit of everything. Now, we began to take assigned roles. My friend Roger became the main DJ, because he was better at mixing than the rest of us. I became the MC, because by now I was more confident and was the best person speaking out front. The rest of the crew consisted of Speng and Little Chris.

We called ourselves After Dark and started hustling for gigs. We played what was known as rare groove. A bit of soul, a bit of old school, a bit of something different. Barry White, Anita Baker, Cameo, Chaka Khan, Omar, Mica Paris. As the nineties continued, our sound became a bit more R&B – Jodeci, H-Town, Mary J. Blige, all sorts. It was a scene that was growing at the time, and one where how you dressed was important. There was a New York American Smooth sort of vibe: slick hair, baggy-line suits with shoulder pads, just a vest underneath. I had a pager, too – these were the days before mobile phones. It sounds crazy, but it was cool at the time.

In the late nineties, the dynamics of the crew began to change: Speng and Little Chris left, and we were joined by Christoss, Mr Fox, Garry and, for a while, Mr McKenzie. We were starting to get frustrated with dealing with promoters and began to promote and organise our own events. The next step from that was to set up our own club. Every August bank holiday for ten years, I had celebrated my birthday with an event called Dons and Divas, which I ran with a couple of friends, Roger and a guy called John Mastro. The three of us set up a club called Virgo's on the Old Kent Road. I learned a lot about business from running that. The

DJing and the music were just part of it – there was so much day to day in terms of the staff and the cleaning, the money, the security, dealing with the council, the police. It was also a challenge as a business model – the only nights that really worked were Friday and Saturday. Which meant you were paying rent during the week, but weren't getting any money in. I also learned about contracts the hard way: the landlord sold the property out from under us to a developer. Even though we'd been there five years, one day we suddenly found ourselves with just a few months to clear out.

I became a partner at a bar in Canary Wharf, where the challenge was the other way round: the bar was packed during the week, with people drinking after work, but quiet by mid-evening and dead as anything on a Friday and Saturday night. I was brought in to do some promotion and fill in the gaps. I lasted about a year: I didn't have the same connection with the people I'd set up Virgo's with, and the whole thing ended up being quite short lived.

Canary Wharf couldn't have been more different to the Old Kent Road. The place was called City Bunker and it was a banker's dream – you could go in there, have a drink and play a round of virtual golf on one of their large simulation screens. Virgo's had basically been a Black club. City Bunker had a different clientele. One time, in there, this guy came up to me, the top button of his shirt undone, his tie at an angle.

You know what? he said. You're the first Black person I've ever spoken to.

I just stared at him. I would say he was a city boy, but I suspected he was the wrong side of forty. What do you say to someone like that? I pulled out of being a partner shortly after that.

Twenty-Two

A few years after the murder of Stephen Lawrence, I was driving with a female friend when someone ran out in front of my car. We were driving through Walworth and Bermondsey. As I've said before, Bermondsey was always somewhere I was wary of.

It was about four o'clock in the afternoon. It wasn't dark or foggy, or anything like that, but this boy ran straight in front of me without looking. I slammed the brakes on – how I didn't hit him, I'm not sure, but he was so close his hand touched my bonnet as I screeched to a halt.

Hey! I shouted.

I got out the car. I was angry.

I could have killed you. What do you think you're doing?

He was a young boy, eleven or twelve or so. Somalian, I later found out. He looked petrified.

Oh, I'm sorry, he said, holding his hands up. It's just . . . these boys are chasing me.

As he spoke, I noticed he was out of breath. I glanced back to where the boy was looking, and saw a group of older white boys running towards us.

Do you know them? I asked.

The boy shook his head.

So why are they chasing you? Are they trying to beat you up?

The boy looked over at the white kids, then back at me. He didn't need to say anything else. I understood.

Wait here, I said.

In my mind, I couldn't help remembering what had happened to Stephen Lawrence. A single Black boy. A gang of white youths. How could you not?

The group had stopped when they saw me. I called them over.

Hey, do you know this boy? I asked.

They were all a bit petulant, shook their heads. One of them was trying not to smirk, which really got to me. I grabbed one of the kids by the collar.

Listen, I said. Don't be beating up anyone because of the colour of their skin, you got that?

I let go of him. Don't ever let me see you doing this sort of thing again, OK?

Then I jerked my thumb backwards: *Get out of here.*

For a second, I thought the group might come back at me. But they saw sense and shuffled off.

I turned back to the young Somalian. Are you OK? I asked.

The boy didn't look OK, but he nodded: I think so.

Well, if you're sure . . . What's your name?

Hamid.

OK, Hamid. Do you want me to run you home or anything?

The boy shook his head: No. No, I think I'll be OK.

All right, I said. Well, take care of yourself.

I got back in the car and watched him go. Then I turned the key and drove off. As I was driving away, my friend and I talked about it in detail. Had I over-reacted? I didn't know any of the background to the story. This could just have been kids being kids. But at the same time, I knew what I'd seen. And the Stephen Lawrence story was fresh in my mind. The possibility that this could escalate into a similar incident was too strong to ignore. The Stephen Lawrence attack had been so quick – the whole incident took, what, fifteen to twenty seconds. There wasn't time to think at a moment like this. You either stepped in or you didn't. Whatever the backstory, I felt I'd done the right thing, and thought no more about it.

A few weeks later, I found a formal-looking letter on my doormat. It was from the police, asking me to come down to Walworth Police Station as they wanted to ask me some questions about something. The letter didn't say what the matter was, and as I read it, I felt confused to be honest, I'd completely forgotten about the incident with the Somali boy.

I turned up at the police station as requested, and they started to interview me about the incident. *OK*, I thought, *the Somali kid must have gone to the station and reported what happened. They must need me as a witness to corroborate his story.*

But the police officer explained it was not the Somali kid, but one of the other boys who had contacted them. He's made a complaint against you for racially abusing him.

When he said that, my jaw nearly hit the floor: Are you ... what? You can't be serious?

Oh, this is very serious, Mr Lawrence, the police officer replied. From what the boy has said, I think we may have enough evidence to charge you with racially aggravated GBH.

Wait. What? There must be some sort of mistake.

I was struggling to get my head round was happening. I said: You're charging *me*? I stepped in to stop a racist attack, and you're going to charge me? This is bullshit!

The whole interview felt completely surreal. It was like I was in a parallel universe or something, where the same set of events had played out in a completely different way. But the police officer pressed ahead, talked through all the procedures and what was going to happen, and I found myself thinking, *This is really happening.* The police officer explained that he was going to investigate the complaint against me, and I would be told when the case would go to prosecution and I'd end up in court.

There's no way that's going to happen, I thought. *Once they look into this, they'll realise how ridiculous the accusations are and the case will be dropped.*

I sat there, and politely told them in as much detail as I could remember exactly what happened. *Once they hear all that,* I thought, *then they'll realise how crazy this is.*

But when I finished, the police officer said, I think we're going to have to take this further.

Have you found the boy? I asked. Hamid? He'd back up what I said.

We did look at his school, the police officer said deadpan. But there were four Hamids there and we only have so much manpower.

How many Hamids did you say there were? I asked.

The police officer looked down at his notes. Four, he replied.

Four? And you couldn't be bothered to find him?

If you're not going to find him, I will, I thought. And so I went to the school, stood outside the gates at the end of the school day. Five minutes later, Hamid came out. Seriously, it was that easy. I went up to him and explained the situation, and he asked me to come back to his house and speak to his father.

Hamid's father was a lovely guy; very humble, very welcoming, very friendly. He couldn't shake my hand enough, was incredibly grateful for what I'd done to save his son. When I told him what the police were saying, he couldn't believe it. The family were trying to make a new life in this country – I don't think this incident was quite what they were expecting.

Of course we'll give a statement, he said. Whatever you need from us.

Hamid and his father went to see the police and gave their

140

statement. My friend who'd been in the car gave her statement too, backing up what I said had happened. At this point, I assumed that would be the end of it. But no. Still the police didn't drop the case. They were determined to push it through and so a court date was set. I really couldn't believe what was happening, but suddenly the whole thing got very real.

The one stroke of luck I had in the whole case was completely by chance, when I was in the gym in Brixton. I'd been going down there to work out, and I overheard a couple of guys talking about Stephen Lawrence.

You're not going to believe what happened to me, I said, interrupting the conversation, and I told them about the incident with Hamid.

Hang on, one of the guys said. You're telling me that you stopped a racist attack, and now they're trying to charge you?

I nodded.

Have you got a lawyer or anything?

When I shook my head, he said, You're going to need a good one. Give me your details. I think I can help you.

It turned out the guy was a member of a campaigning group called Movement for Justice. He invited me along to one of their meetings, where I told the members about the case. They couldn't have been kinder or more supportive. They helped me to find a solicitor and started to campaign on my behalf. They set up interviews in the local press, put together a petition. We stood outside Brixton Tube station, getting people to sign. I felt a bit embarrassed about putting myself forward like that, but they really encouraged me, believed in my case. We've got to get people talking, let them know what's going on.

I asked various people to write character testimonies on my behalf. Among them was a letter from Mum. 'Lee is a kind and gentle person,' she wrote, 'and as his mother I know if there was a fight Lee would be in the middle making peace . . . for his act of kindness he is now in court! I would be devastated if an injustice came to my son from doing nothing as it did to me! Lee is not a violent person. He is a very peaceful, mature and responsible person especially for a young man his age. You don't find young people like Lee these days.'

Eventually, the day of my court case came up. Movement for Justice was there in numbers to support me. Hamid and his father were there. By this point, the police had dropped the claim of racial aggravation but were still pressing ahead with the charge of GBH. So there I was, in the dock, waiting for the case to begin. I was nervous – who wouldn't be? The stakes were high. Although I knew in my heart the truth of what happened, I really didn't know how events were going to unfold. For them to have got this far, it didn't leave me with much confidence that the truth would come out. I was really worried that I had been set up.

The court case began. The white boys were called up to give their version of events one by one. I could see they were nervous, and as they were being asked questions they were stumbling over their answers. It didn't take long for the judge to start intervening and asking them questions herself. When the second boy started giving evidence, it was clear that their stories didn't match up. There were inconsistencies left, right and centre.

The judge called a halt to proceedings.

This is ridiculous, she said. I can't believe this man is in my court. She looked over at me and said, He should be commended for what he did.

The whole place exploded into uproar. There were lawyers up and down like jack–in–a–boxes, but that was it – she threw the case out there and then. I never got to give my side of the story because I never needed to. The judge saw the case for what it was in the first ten minutes and wanted no part of it. I went out into the sunshine a free man, stood on the steps outside surrounded by supporters, had my photograph taken by the press. I was hugely relieved that the whole thing was over, even if underneath I remained furious that it ever got as far as it had.

There was so much about that case that made me angry. There was the assumption from the police, in accepting the original accusations from the boys. If it had been a group of Black boys making an accusation about being racially attacked by a white man, would they have jumped so quickly to action? I'd like to believe otherwise, but I simply don't think that would have been the case. There was something that stuck in my mind about the use of racial aggravation – a charge that had been brought in to protect communities such as mine, but now was being used against us. There was the fact, too, that the police pursued the case in the face of such minimal evidence. As the judge's response showed, it should never have gone to court. So how had it been allowed to proceed?

The fact that it happened in the wake of Stephen Lawrence shook me as well. Rather than encouraging people to step up in potentially similar situations, my story suggested exactly the opposite. Why would you intervene in someone getting attacked when you might end up in court yourself? That worried me: someone else might find themselves in a similar situation and think twice about trying to help.

The very last thing that happened was the weirdest of the lot. There is a photo of me and the Movement for Justice team after the court case, where I'm surrounded by most of the members, but there's one guy who is hanging back, almost like he doesn't want to be there. I was later told that he was an undercover police officer, part of a team sent out to infiltrate what the police considered radical groups at the time – these officers were pretending to be activists but all the while reporting back.

At the time of writing, there's an ongoing public inquiry into this whole form of policing, so I'm limited in what I can say about it. But to have a police officer embedded in a group campaigning for someone fighting a trumped-up charge brought by the police?

That's seriously messed up. What information he was reporting back and to who, God only knows. Thankfully, in my case, such tactics didn't make any difference to the outcome of the case.

The family of Stephen Lawrence had a long and painful journey towards justice. His death not only brought up questions of racism and the threats faced by the Black community, but it also demonstrated the failings of the police in investigating such crimes.

Following Stephen's death, it didn't take long for local members of the community to tell the police who they thought were responsible. Various sources pointed the finger at four particular individuals: Neil and Jamie Acourt, Gary Dobson and David Norris. Having taken a statement from another victim who had allegedly been stabbed by these youths, the police decided to start surveillance of them, despite having sufficient evidence to arrest them. The senior detective leading the investigation later claimed he did not know that he was allowed to arrest individuals on the grounds of reasonable suspicion. Instead, the police surveillance watched the suspects leave the house, complete with bin bags of potential evidence. They didn't follow them because those watching lacked a mobile phone or any other way of communicating back to base.

It wasn't until a fortnight after the murder that the four original suspects, plus Luke Knight, were arrested. Neil Acourt and Knight were identified by Duwayne Brooks, the friend who was with Stephen Lawrence on the night, and charged with murder. However, the charges were dropped the following month, when the Crown Prosecution Service decided that the evidence from Brooks was unreliable. New evidence was then brought forward, but the CPS said it wasn't enough for new murder charges.

In September 1994, a year and a half after Stephen's death, the family launched a private prosecution against Neil Acourt, Knight and Dobson. This eventually took place at the Old Bailey in April

1996, but collapsed after the judge ruled out Duwayne Brooks's identification evidence. The three suspects were acquitted and, having pleaded not guilty, could not be tried again.

Following the collapse of the private prosecution, in early 1997 a coroner's inquest recorded a verdict of unlawful killing 'in a completely unprovoked racist attack'. The *Daily Mail* printed pictures of the five original suspects under the headline 'Murderers' and challenged them to sue. After the inquest, Stephen's mother, Doreen, said in a statement, 'There were times this week when I was not sure whether I was in a courtroom listening to evidence of how my son was killed or at a circus watching a performance. It became a mockery of trying to get to the truth ... The wall of silence was not only in the surrounding area where my son was killed but with the police officers who were supposed to be investigating the crime. Right from the start on the night our son was murdered, it seemed that in the minds of the police he was only a Black boy, so why bother. No one can convince me otherwise.'

The Lawrence family asked the Police Complaints Authority to look into the failure of the police investigation. They came back saying that there were 'significant weaknesses, omissions and lost opportunities' in the investigation, but dismissed any allegations of racism.

In the summer of 1997, after the victory of Tony Blair's Labour Party in the May election, Stephen's parents met the new Home Secretary, Jack Straw. Straw's predecessor, under the Conservative government, Michael Howard, had never met the family. According to Doreen Lawrence, Howard 'had never shown a single ounce of interest in our fight for justice and had always refused even to meet us'. Straw ordered the public inquiry the family had been fighting for, led by Sir William Macpherson. This took place in 1998, with the five suspects forced to give evidence or face prosecution. Macpherson's report was published in February 1999.

In April 2005, the government changed the rule on double

jeopardy, meaning that suspects could be tried for the same crime twice, if there was sufficient new evidence. New forensic evidence came to light, and six years later, in November 2011, Gary Dobson and David Norris were put on trial for Stephen's murder. The new forensic evidence included a spot of Lawrence's blood on Dobson's coat and two of Lawrence's hairs found in evidence from Norris's bedroom. Covert footage revealed that Norris had talked about 'skinning' Black people and setting fire to them. In January 2012, almost two decades after the attack, Dobson and Norris were found guilty of Stephen Lawrence's murder, and effectively jailed for life.

If it wasn't for the tenacity of Doreen and Neville Lawrence, those two individuals would never have been convicted. It's important to remember just how fundamental their efforts were in keeping the case alive. Just as there had been, in my far less significant case, an undercover officer monitoring Movement for Justice, so the Lawrence family also had to deal with the discovery that the Met had tasked an undercover police officer to spy on their campaign and to find out what they were doing.

Like many people, I followed the Lawrence case extremely closely. I would say it was shocking, but with everything my family had experienced at the hands of the police, I wasn't shocked at how events had unfolded. The shock, really, was the other way round – that in the face of extraordinary odds, Stephen's family had finally managed to achieve justice.

Their struggles and determination were an inspiration, and not just to me. After my mum had passed, I found a newspaper clipping about Stephen Lawrence that she had kept. The article had the headline 'The Truth Shall Set You Free'. That was a sentiment I would remember and, along with the Lawrences' spirit, would draw on as our own quest for justice continued.

In later years, I added those very same words to my mum's gravestone.

Twenty-Three

It started with the smash of glass. It was about two in the morning, and I was in bed when I heard the noise. I was straight up and at the window. Out the front, I could see two youths, hooded up, who'd just taken out the front window on the driver's side of my car. I banged the window so loud I thought for a second I might smash that myself. The two youths looked up at me. They looked at each other. And ran.

I was steaming. I pulled on a pair of tracksuit bottoms, a hoodie and a pair of trainers. On the way out the front door, I grabbed a pool cue. I didn't really know what I was planning to do with that, but I wasn't really thinking straight. I slammed the door behind me and headed out to find them.

It's cool and dark and quiet at that time in the morning. I could see my breath, hear the sound of my feet pounding the pavement. *This is crazy*, I thought more than once. But then, to my surprise, I saw them. The youths were checking out another vehicle. I crouched down behind a nearby car and watched them. They were probably in their mid-twenties. One was white, the other mixed race. From the way they were watching the street, they knew what they were doing.

I crept up on them and pounced. I think it was the shock that stopped them. They were so surprised, that in the confusion I grabbed one of them by the collar.

You've broken into my car, I said. You've got two options. Either you pay to replace the glass. Or I'm going to call the police.

We haven't got any money, they said.

Fine, I said. I called the police. Somehow, I frogmarched them back to my car. I kept hold of one guy. The other didn't want to leave his friend in the lurch. We waited.

When the police came, two white officers, they knew exactly who these two guys were. They checked their bags. There were spark plugs in there, other bits of kit you might need to steal a car. The whole thing seemed a slam-dunk situation to me.

The police took me inside and I gave a statement.

You did well to apprehend them, one of the police officers said. But he wasn't praising me. He was being sarcastic, like he didn't really believe I'd done it.

The next day, the police called. You need to come to the station, they said. The two youths are denying that they broke into your car.

I don't understand, I said. You came to my house. You saw what happened. What more evidence do you need?

If you don't come to the station and make another statement, the police officer said, we're going to have to let them go.

I felt really frustrated. When I'd caught the two guys, I'd really wanted to take matters into my own hands. But no, I'd tried to do the right thing and called the police. If I was a white guy, I remember thinking, I'd have been a hero, but because of who I was, because I was Black, their attitude was completely different.

Forget it, I said. I wasn't going to waste any more of my time.

The police let them go.

*

That sort of incident cemented my opinion of the police – that even when you were doing the right thing, they weren't on your side. You were better off not getting involved.

Sometimes, it can feel as though you don't have a choice. There was one occasion when a friend of mine was killed. He was just nineteen and I had just turned twenty-one. He was stabbed in a nightclub his older brother was DJing at, along with a friend of ours. He had asked me to come and MC for him. I remember looking down at the dancefloor below us, the shouts and panic. Everyone was moving, dispersing, running for the exits. I could tell immediately it didn't look good. We sat there until the ambulance arrived, but by then it was too late. There was nothing they could do for him.

When my friend's grieving mother wanted the people responsible to face justice for killing her son, that cut against our normal way of doing things. There was a code in our community, that whatever happened, you didn't go to the police. There was no trust in them – this was playing out at the same time as the Stephen Lawrence investigation, which just seemed to reinforce how little they cared. Whatever the beef, you kept it in the community and sorted it out between yourselves.

My friend's mother, however, wanted to see her son's killers behind bars. So, reluctantly, we followed her wishes and went to the police. I sat down in the station, did an interview, and gave the police all the information I had, but this wasn't much as I didn't see who stabbed him. It was a difficult thing for me to do – I was torn between keeping the code and doing what my friend's mother wanted. I remember coming out of the police station, feeling completely mixed up. Once again, the police themselves didn't strike me as being particularly caring about the case. Although I was there as a witness, there was little sense of me helping them: it was as though we were all the same, that we were no better than the people they were pursuing. All of which reinforced my concerns as to whether we should have gone there in the first place.

The police had their suspects and got their case together. If I felt bad going to the police station, I now felt worse, finding myself going to court as a witness. I felt exposed. Once you do that, there's no hiding from the fact you've been involved. We were compromised and got hassle for it. Friends and family were concerned for us. Are you sure you know what you're doing, Lee?

The case went on, and to the relief of the family, the person believed responsible went down. I thought that was it, but the guy appealed and got the verdict overturned on a technicality. Because of the confusion in the club, it was difficult to determine beyond doubt exactly who was responsible for what happened. Even though I was there, from where I was standing I was unable to see exactly who it was.

Before the guy was released, my friend and I got called in to the police station. From my previous experiences, you can imagine that I was always wary about such a call. In this instance, I was right to be. The officers we sat down with explained the situation with the guy's conviction, and that he was likely to be released from prison soon.

It seemed unusually courteous of the police to give us advance warning. And I was right.

The police officer said, You're both probably worried about this guy's release, because, as we'd been involved in the case, there was a chance that he might try and exact some sort of revenge once he was back on the outside. The police officer offered us a deal. In the courtroom, various accusations were made against people we knew. If we provided them with information to back that up, they would protect us against any reprisals. If we didn't – the police officer shrugged – then they wouldn't be able to guarantee our safety.

We were gobsmacked! The fact that the police were trying to do some sort of deal. The fact that they were essentially threatening us into giving them information. The fact that they expected us to say anything against our friends. The fact that all that seemed to matter was results that ended up in convictions. The case against one guy had collapsed, so now they were going to turn to shopping someone else on the other side of the argument instead. We wanted no part of it, and told them to fuck off!

The experience served to solidify my feelings about the police. Other than the intention of trying to do the right thing by my friend and his mother, I regretted getting involved as it produced no positive outcome. They weren't to be trusted. I felt that I should have trusted my initial instincts about the case and about the code of the community. Because when you did get involved, this was how they treated you. Once again, I didn't get the sense that they were there to protect and help people like me and my community.

After

Twenty-Four

As the discussions over the inquest went on, there was a meeting with Neil Basu, one of the top figures in the Metropolitan Police. Basu is a career policeman – he's been in the force since he joined in the early 1990s and has worked his way up through the ranks, including spending time on the beat in Battersea and Brixton, and in 2013 and 2014 he was the commander in charge of armed policing. He's Assistant Commissioner now, and someone you often see on the news as one of the Met's public faces: he led the operation on phone hacking, for example. I think I'm right in saying that he is also the highest-ranked mixed-race police officer in the force. He had his own battles with racism growing up, so if anyone inside the Met was going to understand our position, it would probably be him.

The meeting was in my solicitor's office in a fairly standard, nondescript meeting room. We both sat there with our lawyers, which, as I was learning, was what you brought to this sort of fight. Neil said he was there to apologise to the family on behalf of the Metropolitan Police. He said that he was aware that the police had never said that, and he was there to acknowledge this and say sorry.

I was dumbstruck. I thought to myself, *Wow, that's quite something. This is, what, over twenty-five years later and you're saying sorry.*

It was a huge deal. But almost immediately, that apology started to peel away.

What exactly are you apologising for? I asked.

At this, Neil and his solicitor exchanged glances. The solicitor was like the other lawyers in the preliminary hearings; I couldn't help but feel he was looking down on me. I got the impression he was there to keep Neil on quite a tight leash as to what he was allowed to say. He picked his words carefully and I got some sort of complicated legal answer, which basically seemed to say, we can't say precisely what we are apologising for at this point because we don't want this to prejudice what the outcome of the inquest might be.

I cleared my throat. I said, So, you're saying sorry, but you can't say what you're saying sorry for?

That feeling I'd had when he first started apologising was quickly beginning to dry up.

Is this something you are prepared to say publicly? I asked. That you've apologised to us?

Again, that look between Neil Basu and his solicitor. No, I was told. At this point, the apology was a private one, just to the family. I became suspicious.

I don't mean to be funny, I said. But until you're willing to make that apology publicly, I'm not going to accept it.

I came out of that meeting not feeling reassured, but like I'd been played. It wasn't a genuine apology, but part of the legal process, part of the game. I got the sense that they wanted to be able to say in the inquest that they'd made the first move, that they'd reached out to us. But the fact that they couldn't say what they were sorry for, or weren't prepared to go public with the fact they'd apologised, belittled the approach. It felt less about justice and more about saving face. It felt mealy-mouthed and begrudging, that we were having to drag the apology out of them, word by word.

The only good thing that came of the meeting for me was the sense that we were on to something. The Met was sufficiently worried about what might come out at the inquest that they were coming to us first and trying to head us off. But rather than succeeding, it just gave me confidence that they felt rattled, and that we should absolutely push on as a result.

I was set to take the stand on the opening day of the inquest, and I was nervous. I'd long since given up my personas of Rudy Lee, Younger Cowboy and Brandy Lee, but I was still getting used to standing up just as myself – getting used to myself being enough.

The inquest wouldn't take place in the boardroom where the preliminary meetings had taken place; we'd be in a courtroom. I wouldn't have much time to get a feel for the place, which would have made me more comfortable – I was going to be thrown right in there, at the start of proceedings. I was acutely aware this was going to be my one chance to speak, to get across what I wanted to say. I wanted to do that right.

The week before, I spent a lot of time at the Bhatt Murphy offices, discussing the case and my statement. The QC representing the family was a guy called Dexter Dias. I liked him from the moment I met him – he had a real presence about him. He looked like a lawyer: the forensic demeanour, the slick hair, the smart suit. But as smart as his suit was, there remained something a bit ragged and rough around the edges about him. A touch of the streetfighter to him, a gloves-off kind of a guy. He was the sort of person that you looked at and thought, I'm glad he's on my side. And he couldn't have been nicer to me – he was so respectful of the family throughout the process and was continually asking me questions: Am I being firm enough? Do you want me to push harder?

Right from our first meeting, I knew he'd really done his homework on the case, and that he was ready to do battle for us.

Dexter took me through what he would ask and what I was going to say. He would highlight potential problems and we would work out solutions. I couldn't help but tense up when he asked questions about Michael.

We need to work this out, Dexter said. Because they're going to ask you questions about him. They're going to paint him as the villain, the bad guy. And if they can wind you up talking about him, then that's going to hurt our case and help theirs.

So we went back and forth over what I might be asked and how I might deal with it.

As the days ticked down, the stress ticked up. On the Sunday evening, I prayed. I knew a woman called Mama Blackwood, who was in a wheelchair. I drove her to and from church every week in my taxi. Mama Blackwood, who has now sadly passed away, was an amazing woman, very warm and gentle, a mother figure type. I called her up and she prayed over the phone with me. I wanted her blessing, wanted any help I could get for the inquest to reach the right conclusion. After she prayed, I felt as though my spirit lifted. I felt relaxed, more reassured.

Not long after we got off the phone, my sister Rose called me: Er, Lee, have you seen what Michael's put up on Facebook?

I had so much prep to go through that I hadn't been looking around to see what was on social media. I went online and flicked over to my brother's page on Facebook. He'd just uploaded what looked like a movie trailer, all about him. It featured a boy running away from the police and seemed to be a short film about the events leading up to the shooting. It was a tease – a 'coming soon' type thing. Here I was, working away for the inquest and there Michael was, using it for his own ends.

I felt tired, stressed and angry. I tried to ring him. I kept working and kept ringing and it was about midnight by the time he answered.

I've just seen your thing on Facebook, I said. Do you know what

I'm sat here doing? I'm going through the paperwork for the start of the inquest tomorrow.

He replied: Oh, is that tomorrow? I didn't realise it was this week.

That just wound me up even more. It had been in the press and all over the local media; how could he have missed it?

I said: I don't know what's worse, you putting up a promotional video knowing that the inquest starts tomorrow, or you not being aware that it's happening – the inquest into the shooting and death of your mum. A shooting that you were also connected with. Please, don't make me waste what little energy I have thinking about you. I've got to be focused here, focused for Mum.

Michael started to reply but I cut him off.

Take the video down, I said. Take it down right now!

OK, OK, he said. I hear you.

That was the last I spoke to him about the inquest. He didn't come to any of it. The only time he surfaced was after the result, when he got his solicitor to ring up and make an enquiry to see if he could be considered in litigation against the police. I don't know, maybe he was worried about the inquest, about what might be said about him in the courtroom. But I didn't have the time or energy to think about what he might be going through. I checked Facebook again before I went to bed and to my relief saw that he'd taken the video down.

Twenty-Five

The night before the inquest was like the night before a school exam. My brain was wired, whirring and talking to itself about what was going to happen the next day. I slept lightly throughout, never really going under.

But the following morning I felt fresh, I felt ready. That sense of yes, *let's do this*. I had the adrenalin going, pumping away right from the start, but in a strange way I also had this sense of calm. The build-up had been nervous and stressful, but it wasn't like I wasn't prepared. I'd put the hours in. That morning it felt like, *finally*. Finally we were going to get our voice heard, we were going to discover what really happened. This is our time, our moment, was how it felt.

I put on my suit, did my tie up. I looked at myself in the mirror. I looked serious. Not to be messed with. I wasn't feeling confident about what would happen, that wasn't quite the right word, but I did have a spring in my step, a sense of purpose. I felt an ease from knowing that I'd done everything I could have done to get us to this point. I felt I'd done right by my mum, and though what happened next was out of my hands, I believed that all of this couldn't be for nothing. We couldn't have fought for this long, had all these wins along the way, without it meaning something. Could we?

We met in a branch of Pret a Manger that was just down from the coroner's court: my four sisters – Lisa, Rose, Juliet and Sharon – and me. Everyone was nervous, a bit lost in their thoughts. Look at Lee, Lisa said, breaking the ice. Always getting the coffees in. What you getting today? A frappuccino, cappuccino, chai latte?

We all laughed at that. And then we walked down together; there's a shot of us that looks like it's from a movie – except I'm holding a takeaway coffee in my hand. But you look at the photo and you can feel our collective sense of purpose lifting off the paper.

As we approached the coroner's court, there were press outside: a film crew, photographers taking pictures. That didn't help with the nerves, but it felt good to know that they were there. That the outside world was listening. There were well-wishers, too. A woman came up to me and introduced herself.

We've never met, she said, but I've lived in Brixton for years and I wanted to come down and show my support for what you're doing.

I was really touched by that – the sense that it wasn't just me, it wasn't just my family, but the community was behind us. The petition had shown us how much support we had, but for someone who didn't know us to come down and be there for us, that meant a lot.

In the courtroom itself, there was already discussion going on between the coroner and the various lawyers. They called it housekeeping. What they meant was that everyone was arguing over the police report and what could and couldn't be used in the inquest.

I wanted to be in there for the discussions from the off, but had to trust Dexter and our team to defend our corner. I had another meeting to deal with: Neil Basu, from the Metropolitan Police. We asked for a meeting with the Met, as a result of them contesting the Domaille report and trying to have it taken out. I was nervous of how this was going to fall, as this was the only solid piece of evidence we had.

I was taken into a private room where Neil Basu was waiting. Whether it was emotion or the coffee, I didn't mince my words.

What's all this about? I went straight in. You've said the Met wants to be able to give a meaningful apology about what's happened with my mum, yet you're waiting until the proceedings are done before you say anything. You can't be fighting us over the process. Either you're prepared to face up to what happened and accept the consequences of that, or you're not.

Neil got it, both barrels. All the tension and pent-up feeling I had in me, I let it pour out. We were that close – *that close* – to getting justice. I was not going to allow that to be taken away from us.

Lee, Neil said. He took a breath. Look. Lawyers are lawyers. They do what they have to do. What I'm saying, on behalf of the Met, is that we're not going to challenge the use of the Domaille report.

That caught me by surprise. I had to stop and do a double-take.

We're not going to challenge the use of the report in the inquest, Neil repeated. We accept it.

What about all those emails? I asked. What about what's going in the courtroom?

Those are the lawyers for the other parties. I can only speak on behalf of the Met. But I wanted to tell you in person that, as far as we're concerned, that report should be included in the inquest.

It's difficult to tell when people are representing an organisation, how much of what they're saying is them, and how much is them doing their job saying what they need to say for the organisation's position.

I'd no idea what had gone down between the Friday emails and the Monday meeting.

But someone, somewhere had had a change of heart.

Neil offered me his hand. I shook it.

*

A coroner's court is similar to a traditional court, but it's not as big. The coroner and the lawyers don't wear gowns or wigs; they're smart, but just in suits. Like a judge would be, the coroner was sitting up high on a stand, able to survey her realm. Directly in front of her were the tables where the various lawyers were sat, piled high with files and notes. As the family, we sat on one side, between the coroner and the lawyers. Opposite us was the witness box, where people would give their statements. Behind us was where the jury were going to sit.

I watched as the jury arrived and were sworn in: out of the twelve people, there were a couple of Black faces, and a couple of Asian or mixed-race people there as well. It felt representative. It's difficult to judge people on first impressions, but they seemed OK, open-minded. It felt as though they'd be fair with us. Because they were behind us, I wasn't able to gauge their reactions throughout the process. Instead I could hear a scratch–scratch–scratch as they were writing notes, and I could hear the silence too, those moments where everyone stopped rustling or coughing to lean in and hear what was being said. Pin-drop moments. There were plenty of those.

Once the jury was seated the coroner began. She was no different in court from how she had been in the hearings: headmistressy, clipped, looking down on the rest of us to remind us exactly who was in charge.

She addressed the jury: You were asked to return for the purposes of the resumption of the inquest into the death of a person believed to be Mrs Dorothy Groce who died on 24 April 2011. Now, the substantive events that took place that have led to Mrs Groce's death actually occurred in September of 1985. It is those events that you will be exercised with and be asked to make findings of fact upon . . .

In her introduction, the coroner set out the scope of the inquest, and how it was there to answer four questions: who died, when they died, where they died and how they died.

163

I must emphasise to you that this is not a criminal court, she said. There is no defendant, there is no prosecution, there will be no verdict of guilty or not guilty. Nor is it a civil court to establish any liability or point fingers of blame. It is a fact-finding investigative forum only.

She outlined a summary of the events leading up to the shooting. How Michael had been wanted by Hertfordshire Police in relation to an armed robbery. How they called on the Metropolitan Police to help them in their search. How the Met had decided to carry out an armed raid on our home address in Normandy Road. How that raid was postponed from the Friday and took place on the Saturday morning. How my mum was shot.

I have pathologist's evidence, the coroner said, that the shooting and the subsequent injuries that she received, rendering her paraplegic, contributed to Mrs Groce's death many years later and it is because of that link between the police shooting and the events that transpired and Mrs Groce's death, that I am required to hold this inquest.

As she asked the lawyers if she'd covered everything, Dexter was immediately up on his feet.

He said, You have, madam, thank you. In summary, if I could . . .

He quickly framed what the coroner had said, dividing the timeline into four sections: the initial Hertfordshire operation on the Thursday lunchtime; the searches for Michael; the briefings on the Friday and Saturday morning; and the raid itself.

He looked at the jury and said: Think about those four boxes. That has helped me, certainly. I hope it will help you to understand the evidence.

Dexter was a smart guy. He wanted to control the narrative right from the off, and he also wanted to make it clear to the coroner that he was going to insert himself into the proceedings. Once again, I was glad to have him on my side.

The first person to be called to speak was Chief Inspector Paul Thornhill. Thornhill was nothing to do with the original police operation but a present-day member of the Met. He was there to read out an extended section from the report. The fact that he'd been chosen to do it – a member of the Met – meant something: they were owning and endorsing the words spoken.

When Thornhill finished reading, there was a silence in the courtroom. It was a long document to be read out and to listen to, and it wasn't an easy one to listen to either, especially for myself. Even though by this point I had seen and read the report, there was still something powerful and poignant about hearing it read out loud in public, and by a senior police officer.

Dexter was keen for the Met to state that they endorsed the report. He was straight on his feet to ask Thornhill to confirm that: The entirety of the document is agreed on behalf of the Commissioner of the Metropolitan Police?

Thornhill replied, It is.

Dexter made him say it one more time: So everything that we have heard you read out is agreed by the Metropolitan Commissioner, for the purposes of this case?

Yes, Thornhill said.

Not everyone agreed with the report in its entirety, of course. Mr Brandon, the counsel for Inspector Lovelock, was also on his feet, to make clear that he didn't agree with the report's findings. Brandon had a bit of swagger to him. His suits were well fitted, he had a pocket square, he was wearing red braces. The first time I saw him, I thought, *you've got a bit of style to you.*

The coroner decided Brandon's concerns were a battle for further on in the inquest: I am sure it will become obvious to the jury when we hear from Mr Lovelock the nature of any objections, she said, bringing the opening session to a close.

Twenty-Six

Mr Lawrence, would you like to come into the witness box, please?

When I heard those words, emotions were boiling over inside me. I was nervous, I was frustrated, I was angry, I was hurt, I was grieving. I was emotional. Listening to the summary of the Domaille report had pulled all of those feelings up to the surface and stoked them. I took a deep breath: I wanted to keep them in check, I didn't want them to spill over.

In the witness box, I realised that this was the one time I'd be facing the jury directly. I wanted to make sure that I looked at them the whole time I was speaking. Lots of eye contact, to make sure they got me, got all of us. I was the only person from our family who was going to give evidence – my sisters hadn't wanted to do it, which was fair enough, and Michael had declined the opportunity to take part as well. The responsibility was weighing on my shoulders.

It was the coroner who spoke to me first. In the morning session, she'd called me Mr Lee, until Dexter had stood up and corrected her. By the afternoon, she at least got my name right.

She said: This is an opportunity to say what it is specifically, what are the family's concerns so that everybody in court can hear what they are and hopefully those concerns will be addressed.

She then asked me to talk through my memories of that Saturday morning. I took a deep breath, and began.

I first became aware of what was happening when I heard a loud sort of bang noise, I said. I woke up and I was still quite sleepy at the time, and I saw my mum walking to the door, to the bedroom door as if she was going to see what the noise was about. At the time, I was reassured that she was dealing with whatever the issue was, so I sort of laid back down and closed my eyes.

Then I heard another bang, which is when I jumped up and as I opened my eyes I saw a police officer holding a gun in his hand and my mum laying on the floor. He was pointing the gun towards her neck. He was shouting out, 'Where's Michael Groce? Where's Michael Groce?'

I was screaming and shouting at the time, saying 'What've you done to my mum? What've you done to my mum?' I just heard her say she couldn't feel her legs, she was saying that she can't breathe and she was saying to my dad that she thinks she's gonna die. At this time, I was screaming hysterically and still shouting at this officer. The officer then turned round and told me to shut up.

As I was speaking, my nerves disappeared. I could feel my emotions as I spoke, but they were staying inside the pot. At one point my voice began to crack but I lowered my tone a bit to temper it and carried on.

Talking back through the incident, I could visualise it, every second. My memory of what happened was crystal clear. The only bit I didn't say, and which I regretted not saying afterwards, was exactly what Lovelock and I had said. The fact I was shouting 'What the fuck have you done?' The fact that he said, 'Somebody had better shut this fucking kid up.' I felt mindful of the space, and where we were, and that it didn't feel right to swear. So I self-censored that part, even though I probably shouldn't have done.

I looked directly at the jury and said: I was ushered from the room. I was with my other siblings and we were all crying and confused and shocked and traumatised at the fact that we'd just witnessed such an horrific event. I remember being extremely worried and I tried to get back into the room. I eventually fought my way back into the bedroom and I looked over to my mum where she was laying on the floor and I saw blood coming from the side of her. I turned to the officer who was attending to her and I said to him, 'Why is my mum bleeding?' and he turned around and said, 'Oh, she's just had a graze, it's just a graze, it's nothing to worry about.' Then I got pulled out the bedroom again.

By the end of saying all this, keeping a lid on my emotions was becoming too difficult. I was remembering a time that had haunted me for almost thirty years. But the coroner was quite brisk in her response and moved the conversation on immediately. She asked me about Michael, and I glanced over at Dexter. He nodded at me, as he knew how I'd react. I took a breath and explained that, at the time, he didn't come to Normandy Road very often at all.

I viewed him more as a novelty brother, I told the court.

The coroner then gave me the space to speak, if there was anything specifically that I wanted to raise so that the court and jury could hear what my concerns were, and what I wanted from the inquest.

This was my moment.

Well, I said, the family's concerns are that we were never part of the criminal trial. So the family has never had the opportunity to be involved or to ask any questions around the circumstances which led up to my mum being shot, left paralysed, suffering for twenty-six years and then ultimately dying in 2011. We only became aware that the report even existed at the time of the inquest, and we only laid our eyes on it in October. That was the first time that we've been exposed to any information around the details of what led up to my mum being shot. So, for us as a family, there's a lot of questions that need to be answered, and we want to get down to the truth around the circumstances which led to her being shot on that day.

As I spoke, I looked over at my sisters, who were sitting there, in front of the jury. They nodded back and I knew that I had done OK. I hadn't prepared what I was going to say as I think I speak better from the heart than from memory. I was pleased with what came out.

I continued: I'd like to say that this incident had a devastating impact on my mum and my family. This was life-changing for us. We've always felt a sense of injustice and we've had to wait twenty-nine years to finally get questions answered around what happened to my mum and the devastating effects that it had on her and our family. My mum was a loving, strong, determined, independent woman and she was mine and my family's biggest inspiration. She's the reason why we are here and I am here and able to talk. I'm just hoping that this process will be able to give her the acknowledgement that she deserves in terms of what she went through and the circumstances which led up to it.

Again, I looked at my sisters, I looked at the jury, and hoped I had done OK. It's difficult when you're in that position to get any sense of that: there's a disconnect between how you perceive things are going down and how they are actually going down. So, inside, I felt tense, praying I was sounding coherent.

The coroner opened the floor up to questions from the various barristers, but apart from one point of order from Brandon, none of the others asked me anything apart from Dexter. Having seen him in action earlier, I knew his technique of asking questions he knew the answers to, but wanted to hear those answers again, to emphasise them to the jury. When it was his witness, Dexter would walk around as well, which you're allowed to do in a coroner's court as opposed to a criminal court. He liked a bit of that, literally holding court, going back and forth to ramp up the drama of the moment.

Dexter said, You have not told us, I do not think, what your profession is. What do you actually do?

169

I explained: I run a taxi company which specialises in a service for people with mobility difficulties.

People with . . .? Dexter asked, just in case anyone in the jury hadn't picked that up.

Mobility difficulties.

With mobility difficulties. As a result of your experience with your mother?

I nodded. I could see some of the jury nodding too. Dexter, I thought, knew exactly what he was doing.

With a flourish, he then produced a photograph of Normandy Road. He asked me to mark our house on it, and also the primary school that I'd just stopped going to, but that Lisa still attended. I made the two marks as requested, and the photograph was then passed around the jury. No one who saw that could have been in any doubt how close our house and the school were.

He asked me again about Michael and when had been the last time he'd stayed at Normandy Road.

I don't ever remember him staying overnight, I said. I just remember him visiting occasionally.

He asked me about the term 'novelty brother'.

He was this bigger brother that I knew I had and I was excited to have, I explained, but I didn't have any sort of relationship with him.

Dexter asked me if I'd consider Michael to be part of my 'core family'. I shook my head.

He quizzed me about Inspector Lovelock's reaction after the shooting: Was he, her having been shot, seeking to help her for her injuries?

No, I said. Another officer came in to assist my mum. The officer who had the gun at no point showed any compassion in terms of what had just happened and what was unfolding and the response to his actions. There's now an eleven-year-old child screaming and shouting and there just seemed to be no consideration, no empathy for that situation.

170

Dexter asked about the aftermath of the shooting. The effect on my mum. What happened to us as a family. And then he paused: You have told us about the impact upon your mother. What impact did it have on you, Mr Lawrence?

I was a bit taken aback by that question. We hadn't discussed this beforehand, and I didn't know he was going to ask me that. *What impact did it have on you?* I was so focused on my mum, and what had happened to her, that I hadn't really considered the effect on myself. I could talk about the effect on the rest of my family, speak about what had happened to my sisters, but to answer directly on the impact it had had on me, that was really hard. It was a personal question, and I wasn't sure whether I could answer it properly. I tried to take a moment. How do you begin to explain how a single moment can change a whole lifetime?

I finally answered: It had a huge impact on me. I'd just started secondary school, so it was [a] very sensitive time for me in terms of a new school, a new environment. When I went back to school, the children were ruthless, they would make fun of the situation, you experienced bullying. My school life suffered, I spent a lot of time at the hospital, didn't really have [a] social life. The responsibility around caring for somebody who's now paralysed and confined to a wheelchair was huge.

Once Dexter had finished, I left the witness box and went to rejoin my sisters. Dexter gave me a nod as I went past. *You've done good.*

My sisters gave me a pat on the back and a squeeze of the arm. *Well done*, they mouthed.

I felt drained, but I thought that was probably a good thing. It meant that I'd given everything I could. I hadn't left anything in the locker, as the saying goes. I'd given my side of the story. Now it was down to others to give theirs, particularly the one person I wanted to hear from more than any other.

Lovelock.

Before

Twenty-Seven

Tony was the guy! He was about eight to ten years older than me and was one of those people who had influence. It was a quiet influence: he was cool, charismatic, had a bit of a swagger to him, with a strong cockney accent. He wore what we called a gold chops – this thick, heavy bracelet that glistened. In the early nineties, seeing a person wear a piece of gold like that gave the impression that this person had money.

If you want the same, Tony told me one time, come and see me. I'll help you out.

I knew what Tony did. Everyone did. If you needed sorting for coke, Es, heroin, whatever your drug of choice was, he was the man to go see. So when Tony offered to help me, I knew what he was suggesting.

Tony's world was different to mine. Weed was part of the culture, part of my growing up. It was so everyday, I didn't really think twice about it. I'd sold a bit to friends from time to time, but weed had always been my limit. Harder stuff, I wasn't interested in. That was more of an underground world, and it wasn't who I was.

But in my early twenties, Mum was struggling financially. I felt gutted about not being able to provide for her and the responsibility of my newborn son Brandon. And the rejection from the job

175

centre with no flexible work left me with no hope. I saw Tony as an opportunity and I thought, *Maybe*. I went to see him, to see if the offer was still there. He gave me a smile and a package. He gave me an idea of what I could make from it, and left me to see what I could do. I sold the package, went back to see him with all the money, which was enough to pay him and buy my own, as I did not want to be indebted to him. He was impressed.

I wasn't comfortable with the idea of being a drug dealer. I didn't see myself as that. It was something I did on the side to provide for my family. In a strange way, I felt a sense of responsibility. There was a code of conduct on the streets and a real sense of your word being your bond. If people bought stuff from me, then they trusted that I wasn't ripping them off or giving them rubbish. I never let it get serious for me – I didn't have any problems from the police or from aggressive rivals or anything like that. I just did my thing quietly and got on with my life.

That's how I justified it to myself at the time. Looking back, I can see it wasn't a good thing to have done. If I had my time again, I wouldn't have got involved. The skills I used in selling drugs, I'd have put to better use. But in defence of my younger self, I'd say this: when I was stuck for money, I didn't have a rich uncle I could call on to bail me out. The only type of people I could turn to for help were people like Tony. So that's what I did.

I didn't think through the effects of what I was doing. It didn't cross my mind, the impact on the end user, or on their families and loved ones. I didn't see any of that: just a friendly chat, an exchange and I was on my way. But the longer I did it, the more the nagging thoughts grew in the back of my mind. I always wanted to be someone Mum would be proud of. And that started to eat away at me. Although I was doing this to help provide for her it was the same thing that could take me away from her and my family. Most importantly, I wanted to be a role model to my son.

I was fortunate. One of my friends was caught, arrested and

ended up going to jail for nine years. Nine years! That was the wake-up call I needed, the moment when I realised it had been my friend who had gone down, but it so easily could have been me. It snapped me out of doing what I was doing and I stopped selling drugs there and then. I made a conscious effort to pull myself away from that lifestyle and start thinking about different ways that I could bring money in.

Looking back now on my involvement, I can see how easy it is to normalise such behaviour, how that lifestyle can swallow you whole, and before you know it, you're in way over your head and there's no easy way out of it. You're then in a situation where things have the potential to go badly wrong. You can end up in jail, you can end up killed. I feel fortunate that I got out of all of that relatively unscathed. I know people who are scarred for life from being involved in that, people with criminal records that have restricted what careers they can go into.

I stuck by my friend who got nine years. I visited him in prison. To me, he was a person first, a human being, a friend, whatever the court said he'd done. I treated him exactly as I hoped he'd have treated me if the situation was reversed. I supported him and he came out, completely rehabilitated, and has gone on to do good things with his life. I'm proud of him for doing that.

Twenty-Eight

After I left school, while I was on the music scene, I became my mum's official carer. Lisa and I looked after her together, along with Sharon when she lived at Mum's, but I had the official title to begin with. Later, Lisa became official carer, while I continued to help. Sharon became more of a companion, reading books with her.

In many ways, being an official carer wasn't that different to what I'd been doing for her anyway, except now I was in receipt of a carer's allowance. I took responsibility for her daily living, her cooking and cleaning, everything around the house. If there was any general maintenance that needed doing, I would either do it or find someone to come and fix the problem. I was my mum's wheels – if she needed to go to the hospital or be taken somewhere, I'd be the person to do it. Mum had a permanent catheter and a leg bag, and throughout the day I'd empty it. When the pain from the bullet fragments got too much, I'd massage her.

Lisa and I worked out a routine for how to lift her. I would lift from behind, do a sort of bear hug manoeuvre to get her into position, and then Lisa would pick up her legs. Between us, we could then carry Mum over to her chair, or out into the car. The older my mum got, the more difficult lifting her became. At

Stoke Mandeville, she'd learned about transferring weight and that helped a lot with the lifting process. But as she got older, she couldn't do that any more. At which point, it was a bit like lifting a deadweight. If you've ever tried to lift someone like that, you'll know how heavy it can be.

A nurse came each morning, primarily to check whether Mum needed any medical attention. If she had sores, then they would dress those. They'd wash and dress her, and then I'd take over for the rest of the day. She needed someone to be in the house with her at all times, so that's what we did. A couple of times I did get all my siblings together and say, look, if we all did a day a week, then looking after Mum wouldn't be too much of a burden on anyone. But every time we tried that system, it lasted for a couple of weeks before someone couldn't do their turn, I ended up covering and the whole thing collapsed as quickly as it had started. So it ended up being back to me and Lisa.

Being a carer is not easy. In many ways, it is one of the most difficult jobs you can do. It requires a huge amount of patience and understanding to do properly. One thing I would pride myself on was how I was able to stay patient and offer my support, however frustrating I found the situation. Like in that moment when Mum swore about the cup of tea in the morning: I kept my calm and my understanding, and carried out the role as best I could. The job can undoubtedly be quite intense and stressful at times – there's a lot of pressure and responsibility on your shoulders. But if you're doing it for someone you love, then it's a job with its own rewards. If I had moments of resentment, it was always aimed at those people who put her there, rather than my mum. No matter how much things felt a struggle for me, I knew my mum was much worse off. In comparison to what she was going through, my struggles were nothing.

I dealt with those stresses and pressures with my outlet being Brandy Lee on the nightclub scene. Carer by day, MC by night. It was a strange sort of double life, looking back, but it did give me a bit of balance, and the space to kick back and unwind. Those two roles would run up against each other sometimes – on a Saturday I'd make sure that I prepared the food for Sunday before I went out, so it was all there and waiting for when I got back. When the evenings and parties went on, there were occasions when I'd go straight from club to caring without having had a wink of sleep in between.

The moments I found most stressful were when I was taking my mum out, or trying to do something for her, and it didn't quite go as I planned.

In 1999 I got my first flat, in Catford. It was in a new-build, everything all white and shiny and new, squeezed in between a graveyard at the front and a trainline out the back. I was desperate for my mum to spend Christmas there with me. I knew it wouldn't be easy – there were stairs to get her up – but I was determined. Partly because I was proud to have my own place and wanted her to see it. And partly, too, because I thought it would be good for her to spend Christmas somewhere different.

I prepared everything. I got the flat sorted, did all the food. I asked Lisa and my sisters to get her ready, so that when I turned up at the house I could put her in the car and drive her over. But when I got there, Mum wasn't dressed.

She says she doesn't want to go, they told me.

I asked my mum what the problem was.

It's too much hassle, she said. It feels too much of a big deal.

It was possibly a combination of my sisters not being patient enough with her and Mum not wanting to put anyone out. I was really upset. I'd put all of this effort in – it was Christmas Day and my plans were crumbling. I was tearful, I couldn't help it.

I just really wanted you to come, I said. I was hoping for us to have a nice day together.

Mum took one look at me and said, OK, I'm going to come.

Somehow, we managed to get her to my flat. It was a struggle, but we got there. I spent the day feeling a bit conflicted, that maybe she felt she had upset me and was doing this out of obligation. But I wanted her to see that these things were possible, and that she shouldn't rule out going to new places just because it might feel too much in her mind. As far as I was concerned, it was never too much. That particular day, the challenge was to get her up the stairs. But I had it all worked out. I had a friend, Garry, there to help me and between us we managed it, step by step, taking a break between each one because my mum was heavy and because the angle was awkward.

I didn't stay in Catford for long. One day, while I was there, my mum called to say that she thought she could smell gas. It was a false alarm, thankfully, but as I drove over to check it out, I came to the conclusion that I was too far away. If there was a chance of something serious happening, then I needed to live somewhere closer. I found a property in South Norwood, which was nearer – nicer, too, a house this time rather than an apartment. Once again, I wanted her round for Christmas. This, I felt, was more manageable. It was a house rather than a flat, and wasn't so far away.

But once she was there, I found myself saying, Do you want to see the upstairs?

OK, she said.

Me, my nephew Aaron and a couple of my sisters started lifting her up in the wheelchair, and quickly realised what a crazy idea this was. There was a window ledge about halfway up that was a real fiddle to get round. By the time we got her up to the top, all I could think was, *somehow, I'm going to have to get her back down again!* We managed that, once again past the window ledge, and got her downstairs. But once we were down, someone said, What's happened to Mum's foot?

It was bleeding. We must have caught it on the window ledge, but because my mum couldn't feel anything, she hadn't noticed what had happened. Initially, I panicked because my mum was diabetic, I was thinking we should get to the hospital. She was OK, but the episode made me realise just how much preparation I should do to make such occasions run as smoothly as possible. It was easy to think about how you'd get someone somewhere, but not how you'd get them back again. What I didn't want was for the situation to feel difficult for her, so then she'd be less inclined to come out and go somewhere the next time. With a bit of foresight and planning, I wanted to show her that anything was possible.

Twenty years ago, disability access was shocking. Sometimes it was OK. Often it was non-existent. I learned to be prepared. If I was going to take her out to a restaurant, I would visit beforehand with the wheelchair. I'd check that the access was OK to get in, have a look at where we were sitting to see that this was OK as well. It was an effort, yes, but it was worth it. To see my mum's face crack into a smile as we sat there, eating a meal together, it made it all worthwhile.

Twenty-Nine

The first time I met Gem, I was twenty-eight. I met her in a nightclub called Sound Republic in the West End. It was her birthday.

She was in the middle of a group of friends, all sat together round a table. The music was thumping in the background. Spotlights swirling round. I didn't know who this girl was, but she was gorgeous. Then I recognised one of the group, who'd been to school with Lisa. I had my in, so I stepped forward.

Hey, I said. How you doing?

Oh hi, Lee, I'm cool.

Who's your friend over there? I nodded to the girl.

The friend introduced me, explained who I was. This is Gem, she said. It's her birthday.

We got talking. Straightaway, I realised we were from similar backgrounds. We'd both grown up in Brixton. We were both from big families. We were both second-to-last children. I hadn't had much luck with relationships recently, but Gem immediately felt different.

I'm doing a club night myself, I told her. Next Thursday. You should come along. I gave her one of my cards, trying to act casual.

Thursday came and went. I spent the night staring out into

the crowd, hoping I'd see her. Kept going down to the doorman to see if she'd come in. But there was no sign of her. Maybe I'd misread the signals. I took another swig of brandy and tried to forget about her.

That was in June. Three months later, I saw her in a club in New Cross called Le Fez. I was walking past and did a double-take when I realised who it was.

You didn't come to my club night, I said.

Sorry. Something came up. But she didn't say it in an unfriendly way, as if she was trying to get rid of me, so I bought her a drink, talked to her some more, danced. We spent the whole evening together. As the lights went up, I asked her for her number.

No, she smiled. You give me your number.

I had this thing in my head where I didn't give the number, I took it. Plus, I'd given her my details last time and she'd never contacted me.

It's how I do things, I said.

Not if you want to hear from me again, Gem said.

I gave her my number.

This time, Gem got in touch. We started texting each other. Then speaking on the phone. I was playing it cool, but things were going well. Then a longstanding booking in Spain came up. We took the club there, went for a week, did different events. I told Gem I'd call her when I got back.

But when I returned, I lost my phone, so couldn't ring her. To make matters worse, I went on the radio. I was messing around with the DJ, chatting about my time abroad. What happens in Spain stays in Spain, the DJ joked. Nothing had happened in Spain, but I laughed and played along. Later I found out Gem, who'd been listening in, put two and two together and assumed that was that.

Months later, in December, I bumped into her at a club called the Scene on Old Kent Road.

I tried to explain: I lost my phone . . .

Whatever, Gem replied.

But she didn't walk away. We carried on talking. I invited her to an event I was doing for New Year's Eve, at the Hilton Hotel on Edgware Road. This time she turned up. The night went well, so much so that I asked her for a date.

OK, Gem shrugged, but with a grin.

It had taken six months, from June to January, but we were finally going to go out.

Fast-forward to the following August. My thirtieth birthday. Gem and I had been seeing each other for six months, and we really liked each other. In the run-up to my birthday, I knew that Gem was up to something, but didn't know what. I found out when I arrived home to one of those suspiciously quiet-sounding houses. I turned the key in the lock, opened the door and . . . SURPRISE! I double-blinked. There was Gem, my friends, my sisters and . . .

Mum?

Hello, Lee, she said. Happy birthday, son.

I was genuinely taken aback by the fact that she was there. Mum didn't travel anywhere without me. I saw the looks and nods between Gem and my sisters and knew that they'd all been in on this together. I knew that to get Mum there was no easy task. The fact that Gem had gone and done it, it meant she really understood just how important Mum was to me.

If we're still together in six months' time, I'm going to marry you, I thought.

After

Thirty

Even though the coroner's tone was brisk and business-like it was my mum's voice that was echoing off the wooden furniture and the high ceilings of the courtroom. The witness statement she gave after the shooting. She explained how she thought the initial noise was my sister Juliet:

'She sleeps upstairs and she suffers from epileptic fits from time to time, and I thought it might be her having a fit and running down to me. I rushed to the door concerned about Juliet and as I put my hand on the door handle to open it the door pushed open. I got pushed back towards the wall between the double bed and the single bed. Several people rushed in and [I] saw that they were police officers. My first thoughts were that they could not be police officers because of the way they had rushed in, but probably that they were robbers dressed in police uniform.

'I didn't notice anything about them because I saw one of them in front of me. He was standing about a yard to the right at the end of Sharon's bed. He was holding a small gun. He was holding this gun with both his hands just in front of his face and was in a slightly crouching position. He was aiming the gun at me. I can't describe the gun. He didn't say anything. The next thing I knew was that I heard a bang and I felt a pain in my left shoulder. I realised that I had been shot . . .

'Lee must have woken at the sound of the shot because he immediately starting shouting. He was shouting, "If you shoot my mum again you will be dead" . . . As I fell, I heard one of the police officers say, "She looks as though she's been hurt". I then saw a police officer over me pointing a gun at me . . . I did hear one police officer still asking, "Where's Michael Groce? Where's Michael Groce?" I was crying out, "I can't breathe, I can't feel my legs. I am going to die."'

When the coroner had finished reading Mum's statement, the air seemed to ring with the silence that followed. She called for a short break. I didn't move. Everybody else filed out and it seemed quieter than normal, as though they were lost in thought as well. I took a moment, then went outside to join them.

Outside the courtroom was a wide corridor, beige walls and wood panels, with chairs down the side for people to sit on. There were lots of people milling around, so much so that I didn't notice him at first. I didn't even recognise him. Instead I saw an old, frail guy, sitting down with a couple of people around him. Then I realised: it was Lovelock. I think he must have worked out who I was, because he immediately looked away. He wouldn't make eye contact with me.

I remember thinking how the roles were reversed. My memory of Douglas Lovelock from that Saturday morning in 1985 was of a tall, imposing figure; a large, threatening presence. I was just a kid, a not particularly big eleven-year-old. For all my bravado of shouting at him, he towered over me, or at least that was how it seemed. Maybe the gun in his hand had something to do with it. Now he seemed a shrunken figure in every sense. Now Lovelock was the one sat down, and I was the one stood up. I was no longer eleven years old, but an adult. Not a boy, a man. The fact that I could look at him and he couldn't look at me back told me everything I needed to know.

We filed back into the courtroom and Lovelock took the witness box. I couldn't take my eyes off him; the whole time he was up on the stand I stared at him, daring him to look at me. But he didn't, not once. He only looked at the coroner, and kept his attention focused there.

I felt the coroner had been hostile to me all along. She couldn't get my name right. But to Lovelock she said, Make yourself as comfortable as possible. If you feel the need for a break do please tell me. Lovelock said he was a bit deaf, fumbled around with his hearing aid. If you can't hear my questions, please do just say, said the coroner. Would you like some water there? Can we provide Mr Lovelock with some water?

My spine felt as if it was on fire. He wasn't the victim.

The coroner asked her questions first. Lovelock gave his career background: in 1985, he'd been in the police force for twenty-one years; he'd been a police inspector for six and an armed officer for three. The coroner asked Lovelock how many times he'd been called out as an armed officer prior to 28 September. He said he'd been on armed operations transferring IRA prisoners to Lambeth Magistrates' Court, he'd been in charge of the armed surveillance of the court, and had been involved in three or four operations involving house searches for suspected armed people. The coroner asked Lovelock whether he'd ever fired his weapon before.

No, Lovelock said. Except on training courses.

Lovelock talked through the training process. The coroner asked him about the planning of an armed operation, and how the system of authorisation worked. Lovelock explained that the planning was down to the officer in charge of the case. This officer would be in charge of the briefing but may or may not be part of the group that went out. The plan of action, too, might be decided at the station or on the scene.

Lovelock said, I should say that the way I'm explaining it sounds very amateurish compared to the methods used today.

You don't say, I thought.

He continued: Looking back, it was in the formative years of firearms, really.

Formative years? It wasn't like the gun was a new invention in the mid-1980s. The acknowledgement of amateurism in describing the set-up angered me as well. Regardless of what time you're living in, amateur is amateur. I found that admission quite shocking: for something as serious as an armed raid, you'd have thought there would be a tight set of protocols for them to follow.

The coroner asked Lovelock to talk through the events that led up to the Saturday morning. For him, it had started on the Thursday lunchtime, when he heard of an incident in Stamford Street: It appeared that some officers from Hertfordshire had gone to an address in Stamford Street, and on their approach to the door a Black man had discharged a sawn-off shotgun, and that the message was coming through that he'd fired the shotgun at the police and they'd run away.

Lovelock said that there was a lot of talk in the control room about the presence of Hertfordshire Police. It sounded territorial to me, that they'd turned up on another force's patch without telling them. It led to the situation where Hertfordshire Police were using their radios to talk back to Hertfordshire, which was then being forwarded on to Scotland Yard and then to Kennington.

It was absolute confusion, Lovelock said. He said the time element with transmitting those messages meant that some of the messages might have got mistaken.

Lovelock said that they subsequently discovered that Hertfordshire Police had been 'on our ground', as he put it, for a number of days, and had arrested and taken people back to Hertfordshire without letting the Met know. He said, The thoughts were at the station it was an absolute mess.

Amateurish. Absolute confusion. An absolute mess. Sitting there, listening to Lovelock's account, you couldn't help thinking that the operation was a disaster waiting to happen, right from the start. Those mistakes at the start were crucial to how the events unfolded. If they'd done their jobs properly and known that Michael hadn't shot at the police, if they'd established that the alleged weapon was left behind and therefore he was unarmed, then the subsequent operation would have been quite different. But because they hadn't established those facts, the impression was that Michael was armed and dangerous, on the run with a sawn-off shotgun, and the police reacted accordingly.

That afternoon, Lovelock along with two of his colleagues went to Haymans Point. This was a tower block in Vauxhall and the police believed Michael might be going to visit a flat there. Hertfordshire Police were already there, and Lovelock's team joined one of their officers who was already in the flat. Lovelock, along with one of his colleagues, was armed. In the flat, they waited for Michael to return. They waited for an hour. Lovelock told the coroner: I stayed there, frightened to death quite frankly.

Michael didn't show. Lovelock was then given another address, this time a hairdresser's on Black Prince Road, that it was suspected Michael had gone to. At about 5 p.m., he led an armed police raid into the hairdresser's. There were two ladies inside, and a white man: no Michael.

On the Friday, Lovelock was told that the police had another address where Michael might be. 22 Normandy Road. He went to Brixton Police Station for the briefing. The original raid was planned for 1 p.m., but the Chief Inspector decided against it, on account of the number of people who were likely to be about. Lovelock said that potential observations of the house were discussed, as well as getting information about the property. But all such avenues of inquiry were dismissed.

Lovelock said: Having worked in Brixton previously, I'm aware that at the time, it was a pretty violent place for policemen to work. Railton Road was almost a no-go area and relationships between the police and the Black community were not good to say the least. White policemen doing observations of that area would've been a no-no; they'd have stuck out like sore thumbs. Gaining information from Lambeth Council was a joke, frankly. The information would be released to all and sundry.

For the police to say, we don't even trust the council to provide us with information – that's shocking. What kind of set-up is that? And to conflate Brixton into this one, homogeneous no-go area was pretty insulting too. Railton Road and Normandy Road are a mile apart. Normandy Road, at the time we were living there, was quite a mixed place. There were white families living on the street. The Cowley estate opposite had plenty of white inhabitants. Normandy Road just wasn't a Black area in the way the police were describing. To suggest that white police officers would have stuck out felt like an excuse.

The coroner asked Lovelock what he thought would have happened if the police attempted surveillance on Normandy Road.

Well, Lovelock replied, if two white police officers were seen carrying out an observation in an area like that they'd have been attacked, simple.

I found that statement outrageous. Where was the evidence to support that? The only time when the police were really under attack was in the heat of the uprisings. Otherwise, who in their right mind was going to see a policeman walking down the street and just attack them for the sake of it? It just didn't happen; it was the community who was scared of the police, not the other way around.

Lovelock was asked what was known about the people who

lived at Normandy Road at the time of the raid. He said that at the police briefings it was suspected that Michael was living there with some of his friends. He said, Somebody suggested it was a squat.

The coroner asked: If it was believed that this might be a squat lived in or occupied by Mr Groce and some of his friends, was there any consideration given to the numbers of people that might be in there?

Lovelock said the police were dealing with up to five men, possibly armed.

Was there any conversation had, any discussion as to whether or not women or children might also be in the house? the coroner asked.

None whatsoever, Lovelock replied.

As I was sat there, listening to this discussion of police tactics, it reminded me not of a law enforcement agency, but gang culture. They were moving and behaving like a gang, on the lookout for a member of a rival gang. In that kind of mindset, you're not really thinking about whether there might be innocent people in the property. There's no due diligence. All you're focused on is your target. All those checks that should have been part of the job went out of the window. I couldn't help thinking that if it was a white suspect they were searching for, would they have the same issue with the council? Did the council tip off everyone, or was it only Black families that they leaked information to? The mindset behind that was disturbing.

My God, I thought, as Lovelock's answers continued. *I can't believe I'm hearing this.* Then I thought, *unfortunately, I absolutely can believe that I'm hearing this.* The more I heard, the more it made sense why my mum had been shot. Such was the mindset of those involved in the raid, it could have been any of us in the house who got shot. Such was the mindset, it could have been any of them who pulled the trigger. It happened to be Lovelock, but in a way he was just the person at the end of a long line of bad decisions, ignorance and opinions based on prejudice rather than hard fact.

The coroner turned to the shooting itself.

Lovelock said that he entered, shouting 'Armed police!'

He kicked the inside door with his foot and went in, in a crouched position: Almost immediately there was this figure upon me and, and . . .

He paused.

I've had thirty years to think about this and my . . . I mean the stress I was under, and I consciously, my finger must've been pulling back on that trigger the whole time I was going up through.

Lovelock was stumbling over his answers at this point: I . . . I was aware of some shout or noise at the same time; it was all so quick. I saw the flash and next thing Mrs Groce is on the ground. And I dropped down to her and I was thinking, *I hope to Christ she's . . . it's shock and I've missed.*

All the time Lovelock was saying this, I was staring at him and he wasn't looking back. *You're really just trying to fumble your way out of this*, I thought, *by making out you sort of went in there and you don't know what happened and the gun sort of went off.* 'I hope to Christ I've missed.'

But I was there. I knew that wasn't his response. His response was, 'Where's Michael Groce?' He wasn't interested in the fact my mum had been shot. He was interested in where Michael was.

The coroner asked Lovelock what else he remembered. His response was: I was in such a daze, really.

Conveniently, he didn't remember shouting at me or telling me to fucking shut up. That's the type of detail I don't believe ever leaves you. I didn't buy his answers. To me, they were bullshit.

All through the coroner's questions, I'd been scribbling notes to Dexter, passing them across. Ask him about this, ask him about that. I could feel my palms getting sweaty, my shoulders tensing

196

up to each answer. My stomach was churning, my anger burning up inside me.

With the coroner finished, now it was Dexter's turn. Finally, the man who shot my mum was going to answer the questions I'd been waiting thirty years to ask.

Thirty-One

I knew as soon as he stood up that Dexter was well up for this. He was a legal pitbull: he wasn't going to let go until he had what he wanted. He played the room, stalking back and forth across the court right up to where Lovelock was sitting and then back over to the jury to press his point home and to make sure they were on board.

First question: Now, after you shot Mrs Groce she collapsed on the floor, did she not? She was screaming, was she not?

Lovelock mumbled a reply.

Dexter wasn't going to let him get away with that: This is quite a big room, so it would help us if you could try and keep your voice up. Was your answer 'I'm sure she was'?

Yes, Lovelock said, a little louder.

It was absolutely obvious after she had been shot and she had collapsed and she was screaming that this is a woman who you had fired a bullet into, was it not?

Lovelock said he only realised that once he'd knelt down and checked.

Dexter was having none of this. That is utter nonsense, is it not, Mr Lovelock?

Lovelock said no, that he was hoping he had missed, and that she was in pain from the shock. He said: The blast was a fearful sound; I was hoping it was from sheer shock. I was in shock the thing had gone off, and I was hoping to hell that it hadn't hit her. I was down there saying, 'Please God it hasn't hit you.'

That's not true, I thought.

This is all lies, Dexter said.

I was in a complete daze, Lovelock said.

Dexter said: Your attitude was one of callous indifference to that lady, was it not? Though she had been shot and was lying on the ground screaming, you said to her, 'Get up.'

Lovelock denied saying this. But Dexter brought up the evidence of another police officer in the raiding party, Dave Edmonds, the man who had smashed the door open with a sledgehammer. Edmonds had said under oath that Lovelock had said 'Get up' after he'd shot my mum. Lovelock, though, continued to deny it.

Not as far as I recall, not the way I remember it, were his responses.

Dexter questioned Lovelock's opinions: We also see your attitude towards the Black residents of Brixton, do we not? You had an attitude of treating them almost as the opposition or the enemy. It was us versus them, was it not?

Lovelock didn't completely deny this: In dealing with certain elements in the Railton Road area when I was at Brixton, there possibly was some of that.

There was some of that, us versus them, Dexter echoed. You believed that this Black man . . . you were going to prioritise finding Michael Groce over the safety of innocent members of the public, were you not?

Lovelock denied this.

Dexter said: That raid was a reckless raid, was it not?

No.

It should not have happened, should it?

Lovelock snapped, I wish to hell it hadn't happened.

That's a different question, Dexter came back. What you wish now is not the question.

The question, he said again, was whether the raid should have happened. Lovelock replied that this was easy to say thirty years later. Again, Dexter didn't let him off. He pointed out the conclusions of the Domaille report, which said exactly that: not thirty years later but from an investigation that began on the same day as the shooting.

You're telling me, Lovelock snapped again. I've never seen the report.

That surprised Dexter. It surprised me. How could he not have seen the report? I wasn't sure which was worse, really: that the detailed report into his conduct was never shown to him or discussed while he was a serving police officer; or that later on, when he had the chance to read the report – we knew from the back and forth with his counsel that his legal team knew the report inside out – he hadn't looked at it. I didn't understand how he could turn up at the inquest without having looked at the report. I didn't understand how he could have been so incurious as to what its findings were.

Dexter had a copy of the summary of Domaille's conclusions that had been read out at the start of the inquest, which he handed over to Lovelock to read. He read out one of Domaille's conclusions, that the decision to continue with the operation was not reasonable, and that grave risks were created for both the police and the public. He told Lovelock that the conclusion had been accepted by the Metropolitan Police.

I'm not sure that I agree with it, Lovelock said.

Dexter put it to Lovelock that, as the raid leader, it was his decision whether to continue with the raid or to abort it. Lovelock denied this, saying that all firearms officers were equal.

Completely untrue, said Dexter. He pushed again. You were questioned by Mr Domaille on the basis that you were the raid leader, were you not?

Mr Domaille called me the raid leader, Lovelock replied.

Dexter wasn't going to let him off the hook. And you never tried to suggest that you had not been appointed the raid leader, did you? You never tried to suggest that anybody else apart from you had been appointed the raid lead.

I took full responsibility for this accident, Lovelock said. It was my fault that Mrs Groce got injured and I take full blame for that, and I'll stand here and take the blame, and I say to the family now I am bitterly disappointed that this happened, I truly am.

He still didn't look at us when he said this.

Listening to these exchanges, his answers were inconsistent. One minute it was 'I didn't want to do this, I was tired'. The next, 'Everyone wants to put it on me? OK, I'm the bad guy.' There wasn't any ownership, or responsibility. It was as if he was just saying what he thought he had to say to get himself off that stand.

'I say to the family now I am bitterly disappointed that this happened.'

Disappointed? *You shot an innocent woman in front of her children*, I thought.

Disappointed? Put it this way: I'm disappointed if I miss my train. His only disappointment, I felt, was the discomfort this was causing him. The fact that he was called back to talk about the incident when he thought it had all gone away. It felt no different to him telling me to fucking shut up all those years before. He made me feel as much of an irritant in that courtroom as I'd been to him back in the bedroom at Normandy Road.

Dexter pressed him on responsibility. When Lovelock was outside the house, did he have the power to stop the raid? Lovelock eventually conceded that he did. Dexter quoted the Domaille report again, that, 'the decision to continue the operation created great risk'. Now Lovelock challenged the report. First, he claimed it was written well after the event (it was completed six weeks later). Then he said Domaille was not trained in firearms, which again was simply not true. In fact, he had much more experience than Lovelock did.

Dexter looked taken aback: You are suggesting Mr Domaille was not trained in firearms? Is that a truthful answer?

Lovelock's lawyer, Mr Brandon, stood up and said that Dexter's questions were not appropriate, and that this was not a criminal trial.

The coroner agreed: I know that it is your intention to press the witnesses hard, but this is an inquest, this is a fact-finding investigative forum.

She asked him to temper his language so that it was less combative. It is not assisting myself, she said. *It's working for me*, I thought.

Mr Lovelock, Dexter said, trying to sound more polite, are you suggesting that Assistant Chief Constable Domaille was not experienced in firearms?

He got him to read the start of Domaille's report, which listed his firearm credentials. Lovelock stopped questioning those after that.

Dexter asked Lovelock about my mum: whether she had a weapon, whether she was armed, whether she touched Lovelock, whether she injured him or aimed a blow at him. Lovelock's lawyer jumped back on his feet again, calling Dexter's questions ridiculous and without any basis in fact. The coroner came in as well and the three had a legal version of fisticuffs about what Dexter could and couldn't ask. Once again, I was glad that I had Dexter as my pitbull in the fight.

Dexter asked Lovelock about what I'd said and seen. That Lovelock had shouted 'Where's Michael Groce?' That he'd pointed his gun at me. That he'd told me to fucking shut up.

I was on the floor tending Mrs Groce, Lovelock repeated to each question.

I knew what had happened in that room. Lovelock knew what had happened in that room. His answers, in my opinion, were a way of avoiding answering the question. He wasn't saying no, but was dead-batting what I'd said.

The questions kept coming. Dexter grilled Lovelock over why the police thought 22 Normandy Road might have been a squat. He took him through the official firearms training manual, which seemed to run counter to the way the raid had taken place. According to that document, because no one's life was at risk, the police should not have tried to break in and arrest Michael. Why was it so urgent? Lovelock was asked.

Because as far as I knew this man was raging around with a sawn-off shotgun, Lovelock came back.

Dexter refuted that: Absolute nonsense. The police had got the shotgun from the Stamford Street property, and it had been taken to Lovelock's police station in Kennington. Lovelock, though, said he didn't know that.

In his final hour of questioning, Dexter began by referring to the fact that, earlier, Lovelock had said that he took full responsibility for shooting my mum.

What did you actually do that was wrong? Dexter asked.

Looking back, I shouldn't have gone on that raid, Lovelock said, because I was obviously so stressed when I went in through that door, and the tension on the trigger was such that it went off.

Dexter quizzed him on this. The firearm had both a single safety and a double safety setting. The latter required nine pounds of pressure to fire a bullet from the gun. That was the setting Lovelock had the gun on when he entered Normandy Road. Dexter took him back through the training manual for firearms officers once again, asking him again whether he thought the raid should have taken place.

I think it's a situation you would be damned if you didn't and damned if you did, was Lovelock's reply this time.

Dexter tried again. He mentioned the lack of information about the inside of the building and who was in it. He mentioned again the training, and the fact that there was no immediate risk to life. Given all that, was Domaille correct to say that the raid should not have gone ahead?

Yes, Lovelock finally admitted.

Having got this admission, Dexter widened out the questioning. He asked: When you are standing outside Normandy Road you are in essence at the end of a very long chain of decisions and operational actions, are you not?

He asked whether Lovelock felt pressure from those above him to get on with the raid. Lovelock said that he had.

Dexter asked Lovelock whether he felt he was in the right frame of mind to carry out the operation. Lovelock said that, with hindsight, he probably wasn't. Dexter went through why this might have been. He mentioned the murder of a man called Clifford, which Lovelock had found out about on the morning of the raid. This was a gruesome firearms incident. Lovelock agreed that it had played on his mind as he turned up at Normandy Road. Dexter took him back to Haymans Point, where he had waited for Michael on the Thursday afternoon and had been, in his own words, frightened to death. A combination of these two events, Lovelock agreed, made him apprehensive, tense and extremely nervous that Saturday morning.

In a perfect world, Lovelock said, I suppose I should have said I shouldn't be doing this raid because of the previous raids I've been on and the way I feel.

To me it sounded as if he'd put his ego before what was right and safe. It came back to my thoughts that this is similar to gang culture, that he was in a position where he allowed peer pressure to get the better of him. He didn't want to step down because he didn't want to lose face. That felt more important than the training and the rules and regulations and everything else he was meant to be following.

Dexter asked Lovelock about the information that he had been given about the original incident at Stamford Street. Lovelock repeated that he only found out the truth about what happened when Domaille had interviewed him after the raid. Dexter pointed out that Lovelock had spent time with the Hertfordshire Police officers when he was waiting at Haymans Point. Lovelock said at no point did they discuss what had happened. I didn't believe that. Surely the first thing you'd do in that set-up would be to ask what actually happened?

Dexter asked Lovelock about a police drinks party he went to on the Friday evening before the raid. According to police rules, if an officer had been drinking within twenty-four hours of taking out a firearm, he had to report it. Lovelock admitted, yes, he had a drink the night before, a scotch and dry and no, he hadn't reported it. Dexter asked Lovelock if he had then been out drinking with the Hertfordshire officers. Lovelock said no, he cycled seventeen miles home to his pregnant wife and never went near a strip club, where the Hertfordshire officers had reportedly ended up. The following morning, he got up at 4.15 to cycle the seventeen miles back to take part in the raid.

When the coroner had finished asking him questions, Dexter said, She asked you if there was anything else that you wanted to say. Do you remember?

All right, Lovelock said.

This morning?

Yes.

Dexter prompted Lovelock again: Is there anything that you want to say to the family of Mrs Groce?

Yes, Lovelock said. I would like to say something to the family of Mrs Groce, although I don't suppose they'll accept it, but as I said many times at the Old Bailey, I'm extremely sorry this happened and she seemed a lovely lady to me when she spoke at court, and I am sincerely sorry, I always have been.

He still didn't look at us.

'I'm extremely sorry *this happened*.' Not I'm extremely sorry for leading a raid so riddled with errors. Not I'm extremely sorry for ignoring my state of mind, which was not the right one to be in when holding a gun. Not I'm extremely sorry for shooting your mother, which paralysed her and changed the whole course of her life, and her children's. 'I'm extremely sorry *this happened*.' Even in that moment, he couldn't accept what he'd done. I didn't feel what he said was heartfelt or that he meant it. Lovelock was right when he said, I don't suppose they'll accept it. I was like, whatever. Your apology means nothing to me. I felt there was no accountability. I felt what he said wasn't genuine.

As the questioning of Lovelock finished up, I felt drained. My sisters were tearful. The events that had been talked about weren't abstract or academic for us; they were about what my family considered to be the murder of our mum. I couldn't ask Lovelock personally or retaliate when I thought that he was lying. What I'd wanted to happen – for him to properly own the situation – hadn't come to fruition. And it was frustrating that, despite all the evidence we'd heard, there was no possibility of a trial in a criminal court.

But, at the same time, I felt a sense of empowerment. My actions had got him here, into the courtroom, to answer the questions I wanted answering, knowing he was extremely uncomfortable. I could look him in the eye, and he couldn't look back into mine. The process had been about my mum. About the truth being heard and the circumstances leading up to her death being properly written into history, as they were supposed to be.

Before

Thirty-Two

By the early 2000s, my nightclub business was doing well, but as that mainly occupied my time Friday through to Sunday, I had time to spare for the rest of the week. The two guys I worked with had day jobs: one was a project manager for an electrical firm and the other was an engineer, and it meant they had extra cash coming in. I wanted that bit of additional income, and from a job where I could be my own boss. So I decided to become a black-cab driver.

Becoming a black-cab driver is hard: you have to become a master of the Knowledge – learning all of the routes and roads across London and the best ways to navigate your way around town. Each day I would travel around London on my scooter, a clipboard attached to the front with the maps and routes I was tracing. London is really a patchwork city, made up of distinct towns and villages, and I loved learning about new areas I'd never been to before. I could be in a neighbourhood where the houses were set back and detached, trees hanging over each one like curtains, then the next minute be heading between tower blocks stretching up to the sky, a melting pot of people around me, as if they're all living on top of each other. When I saw a couple of newer builds nestled between older houses, I'd know they'd most likely been bombed during the war. *Look at the houses on this street*, I'd think to myself. *That'd be a nice place to live.* That opened my eyes to possibilities for my own life, but it left me realising, too, how limited people's lives often are. If you plotted out their daily routes, they're spending all this time in their own parts of London, and never discover these places that are literally just a couple of miles away.

I have bad dyslexia, so instead of writing notes at the end of each day, I'd record myself and listen back to it night after night. Like most people, the process took several years and hour upon hour of hard graft, but I did it: I became a proper cabbie. Both Gem and Mum were proud of me for having achieved it. They knew how hard I'd had to work to get there. Even if Gem's praise was tinged with the realisation that it meant I might now be working unsociable hours.

In a similar way to when I was learning London street by street, now with my orange light on I got to know its people. An office worker, a corporate type, someone coming back from a night out. Quirky, outgoing, creative, quiet, older, well-to-do – driving that cab gave me a real sense of seeing a cross-section of the population. I always found it interesting, talking to people; how often you'd start chatting away and pretty soon those barriers would come down. The preconceptions that both of you might have would disappear. Underneath all of that, people are, on the whole, just people.

There were bits of the job I didn't like as much. Late at night you sometimes had to deal with people who'd had a bit too much to drink; they could be rude, or do a runner without paying. And sometimes, every now and then, I'd feel an undercurrent of prejudice. A white guy in the back giving you a look: *Oh, you're one of those.* Sometimes I'd feel ordered around: Driver, just do this or that. Occasionally, you'd get people who'd argue over the fare. The meter is the meter in a black cab: that's set and there's nothing you can do to control it. Yet you'd get some people who thought that it was rigged, and that you were deliberately ripping them off.

One time I picked up a white businessman, who gave me the look as he got in. Then, as we started driving, he really tried it on.

Your meter, he said. That's going up a bit fast, isn't it?

I explained how the meter worked. You're travelling at peak time, I said. So that's why it's going up at that rate.

But you know, the guy continued, when I do overtime at work, I don't get paid any more money for that, do I? Yet you're not only getting paid, you're expecting to be paid more than normal.

I don't set the rates, I explained again. They're higher because they're unsociable hours. I could be at home with my family rather than doing this. So that's why I'm being paid more to be here.

Is that so? I'm not surprised you're working for these rates. It's extortionate.

We continued this conversation all the way to his house. I kept my cool – I'd driven guys like this before. But he was getting increasingly shirty. I couldn't work out if it was deliberate or just for effect, to set up an excuse for him not to pay. But when we got to the address, he told me he wasn't going to cough up. That I'd been trying to rip him off, that I'd been rude to him throughout, that he had a good mind to report me, so let's just leave it there and call it quits. It was one of those toss-ups about how far you're prepared to take it. Was it worth the aggro over a single fare? And if I did take it forward, who would they believe anyway – a Black cabbie or a white businessman in a suit? The last thing I wanted was to get into trouble and find myself suspended or my licence under threat. It was the type of conversation where a lot of stuff is being left unsaid and yet you know exactly what the other person is saying. I shouldn't have done, but I let it go and told him to fuck off out of my cab. It wasn't worth it, even though it was.

Those sorts of people were the exception. Until someone stepped into your cab, you didn't have any idea what they were going to be like, and once you started down the route of not stopping for some people based on what you *think* they're like, that says a lot more about you than about them. Recently, I was up in north London and I was late for picking up my daughter. I saw a cab approaching, light on, and I put my hand out to hail it. The cab driver slowed down, saw me, then pretended he hadn't and drove on. He didn't stop, have a conversation and then decide he didn't want to go south of the river or anything. All I can guess is that he saw I was Black and decided I was trouble. I was never like that – I treated everyone the same, and for the most part, that reinforced my belief that people, for the most part, are fundamentally OK.

The seeds of my mobility business were planted in 2006, at my wedding to Gem.

There was enough to worry about, getting married, but I had an extra concern on my wedding day. Mum. Apart from my surprise thirtieth birthday, which Gem had organised, this was going to be the first time that Mum had travelled anywhere without me. I was worked up about that. How was she going to get there? Was it going to run smoothly? As the wedding approached, I thought to myself, if only there was a company that specialised in this. I would pay anything to have that peace of mind. In the end, I paid for a carer and found a black cab, which was actually painted white, with ramps to get her there.

When I arrived at the church and saw her sitting there, I relaxed. OK, I thought, I can breathe now. As it turned out, I couldn't quite. I had asked my brother Michael to take care of Mum but halfway through the evening he came and found me.

Yeah, I'm going now, he said. I've got a gig.

What do you mean, you're going? I was too stunned to be angry. You said you'd look after Mum.

Michael left. And left me to deal with Mum. At the end of the night, Gem and I had to take her home. Between Lisa and I, we carried her back, into the house, lifted her into bed. Mum was apologetic – but it's your wedding night – but it wasn't her fault. I wanted to make sure that she was OK.

I'd been black-cabbing for a while, when I had a call from a friend, Wayne, about a work opportunity. He knew about everything I'd done looking after Mum and thought it might suit me.

There's an advert on Gumtree for people who want to do disability work, he told me. You should give them a call.

I started working with them, taking children with disabilities to school. I enjoyed it. It felt more rewarding, getting to know people on a regular basis, than just picking up strangers. I searched for similar work and joined a circuit called ComCab. They ran a Taxicard scheme, where people with disabilities could have subsidised journeys in black cabs. I got a lot of work with disabled passengers. Again, I found it rewarding.

Later, after Mum passed, I found that I missed the caring. I'd gained all this learning and knowledge through looking after her that it seemed a waste not to try and use that experience. That was where the seed of the idea about Mobility Taxis bore fruit. What if I set up a specialist taxi service for people in a similar position, where the journey was just as much about the patient's care and dignity as it was about getting them from A to B?

I printed a load of flyers and distributed them around care homes, day centres and hospitals. By the end of the first week, the phone started to ring off the hook. To begin with, I was a complete one-man band. It was me answering the phone and then me being the person doing the job as well. With the work there, I spoke to a couple of other black-cab drivers about what I was doing, and they were happy to come on board.

As the business expanded, I brought in some adapted vehicles for community transport and hired dedicated drivers for them. This allowed us to be more consistent and more responsive. Black–cab drivers are good, and the ones we use are all wheelchair-friendly vehicles, but they balance the workload with other jobs. At the time of writing, we've got five adapted vehicles and twenty-five black cabs we use on the circuit. As the business grows, the plan is for these numbers to be reversed. In five years, the dream is to build this into a subsidised community transport service – a fleet of converted cars and minibuses. If we could achieve that, that would be amazing.

Thirty-Three

By the spring of 2011, Mum was sixty-three. We'd got into a routine where I'd usually go and see her every few days. Unless I was away, a week would never go by where I didn't call in. Reading had become Mum's big passion. She read a lot of spiritual books and also ones about Jamaican culture and conspiracy theories. There was always plenty to talk about when I went round.

Mum ended up in hospital so many times – because of an infection caused by her catheter or a bad pressure sore or for operations on her legs – that it got to the point that I almost didn't think anything of it. It was part of the routine, of what her life was made up of. She'd stay there for a few weeks or a month and come back out again. Then, a few months later, she'd go back in. I have three thick folders of hospital records.

That spring, Mum got what seemed like an infection. I was familiar with the signs by now: she'd be slightly delirious – dozy, or speaking without making sense; sometimes she would hallucinate or start seeing things. Lisa would call me up and we'd rush her to hospital and usually they'd put her on a drip and that would sort it out. They'd take the opportunity to check her out while she was there, and as long as all was OK, she'd be back home once the infection had cleared up.

To begin with, this felt like just another one of those episodes. I took her to the hospital, left her in the doctors' hands and went home unfazed. But this time, rather than getting better, she started to get worse. Late one evening Lisa called to say the hospital had called her. Mum had had a turn and there'd been a moment when she'd become non-responsive.

Lisa and I rushed down there. The doctors were unsure what to do and were debating whether or not to take her over to the intensive care unit. Eventually, they decided that they should send her there. They put a tube in her mouth and started to monitor her whilst they ran tests to establish the problem; most likely a chest infection or some sort of pneumonia that her body was fighting.

After spending some time in the ICU, Mum started to come around. I relaxed. A little. It seemed like she was starting to make a recovery, but at the same time, when I spent time with her I could tell that something wasn't right. A few days later, she declined again, and Lisa and I got a message that the doctor wanted to speak to us. As soon as I arrived for that meeting, I knew immediately from his expression that the situation was serious.

The doctor took Lisa and me into his office and shut the door.

I'm afraid to say that your mother's kidneys are failing, he said. It's possible that we could do an operation, but if we do that, then she's going to be on dialysis for the rest of her life. And if I'm being honest, we're not even certain that the operation would be successful.

The shock of that news. Because she'd been in hospital so many times, I took it for granted that each time she was going to be OK.

What do you think she would want? the doctor asked me.

The strangeness of being asked that question. I'd spent so much of my life looking after my mum, but it still felt so foreign to me. That I had to make a decision about the end of her life, when she was the person who'd created me, who'd given me mine. A cruel sort of symmetry.

About a week and a half earlier, I'd been to visit her. We'd been talking about my children, when she'd turned away and looked out of the window. What she was looking at, I don't know, but she said: Lee, I just want to be free.

Exactly like that. I didn't really respond, didn't really know what to say. But I remember afterwards walking back down the hospital corridor and thinking to myself, *I've never heard my mum say that*. Through all the years and everything she'd been through, through all the hospital appointments and visits and stays, she had never once said anything similar. She had always been so strong in her spirit. So the fact that she was speaking in this way pulled me up. Looking back, I think she must have known before the rest of us that this time, the situation was different.

So when the doctor asked me that afternoon what I thought she would want, I already knew what her answer would be.

Mum died on 24 April 2011. Easter Sunday. Her children and some of her grandchildren were at her bedside.

We have a tradition in our culture called Nine Nights. As the name suggests, over nine nights, people came together at Mum's house, where we drank, played music, sang hymns, ate food, played dominoes, talked and shared memories. Nine Nights is a time to remember and to celebrate the life of the person who has passed.

On one of the nights, some of my gran's church friends came round to pay their respects, and they asked to pray for us. Me, my sisters and my Aunt Lorna all gathered in Mum's room. As the pastor started to pray, someone got the giggles. It was infectious. I looked round and could see everyone's shoulders going as they tried not to laugh.

Lord forgive them, the pastor said. For it hasn't hit them yet.

That just made everyone laugh the more. I don't think it was the pastor's intention, but in that moment, there was a real togetherness, a shared moment of relief. Mum might no longer be there, but looking around the room, I knew we had each other.

After

Thirty-Four

The inquest went on for another two weeks. Each day, a succession of police officers involved in the operation were questioned. Inspector Lovelock had been the person I'd been particularly keen to hear from, but the range of witnesses reinforced the sense that, while he'd been the one to pull the trigger, the operation behind the raid had been riddled with mistakes, incompetence and underlying prejudices about the Brixton community.

On Tuesday 8 July 2014, the various counsels gave their closing statements, and the jury was sent to start their deliberations. And then we waited. The jury were sent home that evening, reconvened the following morning, spent another day deliberating and then were sent home again. Each day, we met in a small meeting room at Southwark Coroner's Court: my sisters, my wife, Michael's two daughters, my cousin Kwaku and me cramped around a table, Dexter and other members of the legal team coming in and out to see how we were doing. Nobody said much. Most of the time we were lost in our thoughts. Occasionally, someone would say, I hope we get the right result. Or, I miss her so much. Then we'd nod at each other and go back to our thoughts.

With us in the room was a guy called Simon Jones, who was there to help us deal with the media. Simon had been introduced to us through the father of one my wife's friends. He worked for a company called Chime Communications. He dealt in what was called reputational management. Towards the end of the inquest process, Simon had started coming down and helping out. He handled the interviews with the various TV and newspaper journalists. He helped us, too, in planning what we were going to say. Once the inquest was over, we wanted to make a statement as a family on its findings. But we didn't know what those findings were going to be. We had to plan for various scenarios. That wasn't easy. What would happen if we worked out our response to the verdict that we wanted, only for it to go the other way?

10 July was a Thursday. It was warm, low twenties, a mixture of sunshine and clouds. We'd all been quiet; there was little left to say, and the tension had been building every hour that passed until the air seemed to be static with it. And then an assistant from the court came in to tell us that the jury had reached a decision. The release was palpable. It had taken over three years since my mum had died for us to get to this point – all of that climbing, all the dodging of obstacles, all the reasoning and arguing and pleading to get our side of the story out was finally over. Finally we were at the mountain top.

Before we went in, we prayed. I spoke about the journey, where we'd come from, what the verdict meant for us all. I prayed for Mum's spirit to be with us and to guide us in the hours ahead. We sat silently for a moment more, and then we filed back into the courtroom that we were now so familiar with. As the jury also filed in, I tried to work out their expressions and what they meant, but I couldn't. Now we just had to wait and see.

Members of the jury, the coroner said. I have been passed a copy of the decisions that you have reached.

She asked for the foreman to stand: Now, you were charged with answering the four questions of who died, when, where and how.

I closed my eyes. My palms were sweaty and I clenched my hands together. My heart was racing and my mouth was dry.

Can you tell me the name of the deceased that you have determined upon? the coroner asked.

Mrs Dorothy 'Cherry' Groce, the foreman replied.

And in answer to the question of when and where Mrs Groce died, how do you answer that?

Mrs Groce was shot by police on 28 September 1985 at 22 Normandy Road, which resulted in paraplegia and medical conditions leading to her eventual death on 24 April 2011 at King's College Hospital, Denmark Hill, Camberwell, London.

Thank you.

The coroner paused. She went on: Now, turning to the fourth question, of how Mrs Groce died, you were set a number of questions.

The coroner explained that she was going to read out each particular question and ask the foreman to give the jury's answer to each one. This was the moment. The questions of the who, when and where were a given. But these 'how' questions were what the inquest had been all about. I shut my eyes tighter still, and listened.

The coroner began: Was there a failure to communicate among the police officers in the search for Michael Groce accurate information as to whether by the failure of the first briefing Michael Groce was no longer wanted by the Hertfordshire Constabulary for an offence of armed robbery?

Yes, the foreman said. There was a failure.

Was there a failure to communicate among the police officers involved in the search for Michael Groce accurate information as to whether or not Michael Groce had fired a shotgun at or in the presence of officers from the Hertfordshire Constabulary?

Yes, the foreman repeated. There was a failure.

Was there a failure to communicate among the police officers involved in the search for Michael Groce accurate information as to whether the shotgun seen in the hands of Michael Groce at Stamford Street was recovered by Metropolitan Police offers at that address?

Was there a failure to make adequate enquiries about the occupants of 22 Normandy Road before the implementation of the planned surprise forced entry armed raid?

Was there a failure to make the officers attending the briefings aware that the names of three women, including that of Mrs Groce, appeared on the electoral roll in connection with 22 Normandy Road?

Was there a failure to consider whether women or children might be present in Normandy Road?

Was there a failure to make adequate observations of 22 Normandy Road before the armed raid took place?

Was there a failure to call off the armed raid at the briefing on 28 September at Brixton Police Station?

Yes, the foreman replied. Yes, there was a failure. The only question that the jury didn't agree on was whether the armed raid should have been called off by the entry group itself. For each and every one of the other questions, the jury found there had been a failure.

As each question was read out, I felt myself hanging on for the answer. And as each answer was given, I found myself hanging on for the next one. I could hear the clenched 'yes' of our friends and family as the momentum climbed and climbed.

The coroner asked if the jury had been able to reach a conclusion. The foreman said yes, and read it out: Mrs Groce was shot by police during a planned surprise forced entry raid on her home and her subsequent death was contributed to by failures in the planning and implementation of that raid.

It's hard to describe exactly how I felt on hearing those words. Everything we'd fought for, had hoped for, had come to fruition. And it was a gift for my mum – it was the greatest gift that, in her absence, we could give to her. I felt a huge swell of gratitude towards the jury and the conclusion they'd reached. They would never know what they'd done with those words, what they'd helped us to achieve: the recognition of what we'd been fighting for. The nearest I could describe it was if someone had been imprisoned for a crime they hadn't committed and then, years after the fact, they'd finally got the proof of their innocence.

It was a bitter-sweet victory. The inquest process had been such a draining one: listening to the evidence, and then the waiting while the jury had made up their minds. The case had stirred up heartache, grief, fear and anger, and taken me back to that Saturday morning all those years ago. That was hard. And so I felt relief, and satisfaction, but not joy or excitement. Mainly, I was sad that it had taken so long to get to that conclusion.

As soon as the jury's conclusion was read out, Dexter was on his feet: It is common knowledge that the shooting of Cherry Groce is a tragedy. It is a tragedy that has starved a family, a community and a nation. The decision of this jury places on public record after twenty-nine long years the fact that the shooting of this unarmed woman in her home in front of her children was caused or contributed to by a series of serious failures by the Metropolitan Police. What we have accomplished in this courtroom is a vindication of the inquest jury system, because what this case unquestionably demonstrates is that the truth can and must come out. Even if it takes twenty-nine long years, the truth matters.

The coroner read out a couple of prepared statements: one from Hertfordshire Police and one from the Met. The gist of both was that policing had changed since 1985 and what happened then could not happen now. There were better procedures, and independent investigative systems in place. I later had a conversation with one police officer who told me that in this day and age, thanks to things like Freedom of Information there'd have been no way we'd have had to wait so many years for that report. I came back to him: yes, maybe, but at the same time I wondered if the report would have then been the same. If you knew the report was likely to be made public, you might be more cautious in your findings. Because the Domaille report had been an internal one, I wondered if it had been more honest and scathing in its assessment of the Met's behaviour. And if Domaille hadn't been so direct in his findings, the inquest jury might not have reached the conclusion it had.

The coroner wrapped the inquest up. There was a sense, for me, that we hadn't just won in our battle against the police, but that we'd won against her as well. All the way along, she had tried to curtail proceedings, had made us feel like a thorn in her side. All of my challenges in the preliminary hearings that had irritated her so much: now they had been vindicated. I felt her tone was slightly different towards us at the end as if, finally, she had a little bit of respect for us.

As the inquest broke up, I hugged my sisters and my family. I thanked Dexter and all of the Bhatt Murphy team. Then I went over and shook every member of the jury by the hand. It is hard, in a simple handshake, to emphasise exactly how much their decision meant to me. But I wanted to look each of them in the eye and say thank you for what they had done.

Somebody had better shut this fucking kid up. In 1987, Labi Siffre released a song called '(Something Inside) So Strong'. The song was originally inspired by Siffre watching a TV documentary about apartheid South Africa, which showed footage of a white soldier shooting indiscriminately at a crowd of young Black people. It's a song about injustice and discrimination, but also about the fact that no matter what might be thrown at you, you can rise to the challenge. In the second verse, Labi sings, 'The more you refuse to hear my voice, the louder I will sing.'

Sometimes it takes thirty years, sometimes it takes pain and suffering and heartache. Sometimes it takes legal battles and 130,000 signatures and MPs. But sing loudly enough and one day they will hear you.

Thirty-Five

The High Court is the pale grey, gothic palace of a building on Fleet Street which is often on the news. Walking through the entrance, with its mighty arch squished between turrets, feels like walking into a cathedral. Courtrooms always feel a bit like walking onto a TV set to me. This felt bigger and grander and older than the coroner's court. Even if the specific courtroom where our case was to be heard was one of the smaller civil ones.

It was a couple of years after the inquest had concluded and we were here because the negotiations between us and the Met had broken down. After the inquest came discussions about accountability and the subsequent reparation we were owed. After the verdict of the inquest had been reached, the Met Commissioner, Sir Bernard Hogan-Howe, had released a pre-recorded statement for the media:

Today, I apologise unreservedly for our failings. I also apologise for the inexcusable fact that it has taken until now, for the Met to make this public apology.

To us, the family, he said: I am sorry for the years of suffering which our actions and omissions caused to your family ... Mrs Groce bore her suffering with dignity and her story is a powerful reminder to all officers of our responsibilities when we use force, or plan for its possible use. What is clear is that in this case we, as an organisation, failed to meet those responsibilities and in doing so caused irreparable damage to a mother and her family.

But, over time, things had soured. When Hogan-Howe came to apologise to us in person, dressed up in all his uniformed finery, he read out the statement again, word for word. I tried to make clear what this apology and what Neil Basu's previous attempt had failed to do: neither claimed accountability. Hogan-Howe said he couldn't be the one to make a decision on that; he needed to refer to the 'decision-makers' and the Mayor's Office.

More negotiations followed – we desperately didn't want to end up in another legal battle – but we couldn't seem to move forward. As far as the Met was concerned, the central issue was money. The *only* issue for them seemed to be money. *What do you want? How much do you think you should get?* The Met line seemed to be to offer as little as possible, with the caveat that if we didn't take it, then we'd go to court and might end up with nothing. That, though, wasn't where we were coming from. The central issue for us was for the Met to take into consideration the damage that had been caused – an acknowledgement of this, and some suitable form of reparation.

Eventually, we received a letter from the Met's solicitors telling us that they weren't willing to take things any further and that they didn't think we had grounds to push them to accept accountability or liability. If we wanted to pursue this further, then we'd need to go through the official channels; the courts, in other words.

Once again, I found myself in the situation of putting in the prep: we had all the original evidence, plus a whole load of new material to justify our case. So we went back into battle – me, the family and our legal team on one side, and the Met and their legal team on the other. This time there wasn't a jury or a coroner but a judge, sat in front and above us, with robes and wig firmly on.

As soon as our barrister began to present the case, the judge interrupted him.

Hold on a minute. He turned to the Met's legal team: So, just let me get this clear. You're challenging them? This incident happened, it's been through the inquest process, you've apologised and now you're saying that you don't think you have any duty of care?

The Met's legal team stumbled over their reply: Well, er, you know, er . . .

The judge asked the Met's team whether the force took responsibility.

Yes, was the reply. Yes, but we don't take responsibility for all the things that they're bringing to us.

This was news to us. Up to this point, the Met had not really given us any indication of accepting any sort of liability. Now they were saying they would be accountable for some things, but not others. If they'd made this concession earlier, we would never have had to go to court.

The judge continued to challenge their legal team. It was as if we were watching a headmaster giving some kids a good grilling. He turned to our barrister and asked what we thought. Our barrister said that the Met had never given us any sense that they were willing to accept any accountability. Our barrister asked for time to speak to us, to discuss what we wanted to do.

The family and I left the courtroom, went to the canteen and had a meeting with our legal team. If we accepted the list of things that the Met were willing to be accountable for, then the process could move forwards.

One of the sticking points was whether Lovelock had pointed his gun at me. The Met's position was that they didn't feel they should be accountable for this, because essentially it was my word against theirs – the only corroborating witness was my mum, and she was no longer with us to testify. It wasn't strong enough legally, they argued, for them to justify being accountable. There were a couple of points like this where, if we were willing to drop them, we could go on.

This was difficult for me. I knew what had happened and so on one level it felt wrong to remove that from the list of accusations, as it was true. But at the same time, I didn't want to jeopardise the whole process. I was there to represent the family and what I didn't want to do was to stand firm on this particular point that was about me and run the risk of my sisters losing out as a result.

Everyone was really supportive. The conclusion was that it was up to me, and if I wanted to pursue the Met on that point, then they would stand by me. If it had just been me, it would have been different. But it wasn't, so I agreed to have that detail removed. Having reached an agreement over what the Met was accountable for, there was no need for any further hearing. The judge said afterwards that he was disappointed – that he had been looking forward to the case, as he thought it was the sort of landmark case that would have been referred to for years to come.

Thirty-Six

When she was younger, my eldest daughter Harmony Leigh Lawrence had this phobia of sirens. Every time she heard one, she'd start to worry and panic. She thought something really bad must have happened. I talked to her school about it and they dug out this series of books about the emergency services. That seemed a good idea. She could read about the fire brigade and all the different things they did. Nice stuff, like rescuing a cat from a tree. Suddenly the sirens didn't seem quite so bad after all.

One day, I got in from work to see Harmony reading. *That's good*, I thought.

Hey, I asked. What's that book you're looking at?

Harmony held it up to me proudly. It's all about the police service, she said. I've read about ambulances and about firemen. Now I'm reading about the police.

Now there was a siren going off in my head.

The police do so many amazing things to keep us safe, Harmony said.

I had a freeze moment. What should I say to her? She was too young to know what had happened to her grandma back in 1985. I hadn't had that conversation with her yet. How did I balance the message she was reading in the book with my family's experiences with the police?

With my younger daughter, Ruby-Lee Cherry Lawrence, I found myself facing the opposite problem. We'd been out together and on our way back home had pulled into the petrol station to get some fuel. As we got out of the car, there were a couple of police officers on the forecourt, walking through. One of them nodded at Ruby-Lee as she went past, and smiled. Hello, he said. My daughter just looked at him straight-faced and didn't say anything.

When we drove away, I turned to Ruby-Lee and asked her what had happened.

You know when that police officer said hello? Why didn't you say hello back?

I don't like police officers, she shrugged.

That took me as much by surprise as Harmony's reaction.

Why's that?

They just scare me. My daughter wrinkled her nose. They carry guns around and they're like a big gang.

I double-blinked. The way my daughter was talking, she made them sound like the mafia.

As we drove home, I racked my brain. Wow, I thought. Ruby-Lee had never had an experience with the police but already, at seven years old, she was viewing the police in a bad light. It was exactly the same with Harmony, but the other way round.

I didn't want my daughters growing up thinking all policemen were bad. But equally, I also didn't want them growing up thinking all policemen were good either. That blanket description either way was unhelpful. I needed them to understand that behind the uniform, they were just people, like the rest of us.

But I knew from my own life that your own personal experiences shaped how you felt about the police. My daughters hadn't had those first experiences yet. I felt that, as a father, I needed to prepare them for when that happened. Quite how I would manage that, without their judgements being clouded by my own experiences, I wasn't sure. Not for the first time, parenting seemed harder from the inside looking out, than from the outside looking in.

Thirty-Seven

Another day, another meeting room. This time we were in a barrister's chambers in the Temple area of London. It was one of those areas where you walk down narrow cobbled streets, with grand old buildings towering up on each side, but once you are through the door, you find yourself stepping into something much more modern. The meeting room was all glass, frosted so you couldn't see in. It felt light, spacious, silent.

The meeting felt like a mafia sit-down, where you have the two competing sides brought to the table. We were along one edge, they faced us from the other. Alongside me, my sisters and Gem was our legal team, including a barrister and a QC. I wanted Gem to be present, partly for support, but also to make clear to the police the effect that all of this had had on my personal life. The face of the Met was Neil Basu. He was flanked by his own team of lawyers. In numbers terms, there were more us than them in the room. It didn't make any difference to the argument, but psychologically that felt good. It showed our strength, and our togetherness.

The Met's legal team had attempted to undermine that. In the run-up to the meeting, they'd sent over a proposed settlement with different amounts for each of us. That felt deliberately divisive to me and it created tension between us, which I think had been its intention. Some of my sisters wanted to accept what was on the table, some were confused as to why they'd been offered more or less than others.

Listen, I said to them, when we met up to discuss. Have you trusted me up to this point? Have I got us this far?

When they nodded, I said, OK, well then, I say that we're not buckling now. We're going to go in and do this collectively. We're not going to go down this route where they try to split us up. It wasn't an easy decision – the settlement offers came with the kicker that if they weren't accepted, they would be withdrawn. And there was no guarantee that we'd end the mediation process with the same amounts. The letters put this all down in legalese – take the money now, or take the chance of ending up with less, or even nothing at all. My instinct was this was the lawyers playing games: if this was the first offer, it was unlikely to be the last.

At the head of the table sat the mediator, who was there as a facilitator to help our two sides achieve a positive outcome. Dame Janet Smith was a former judge and had worked on both the Harold Shipman and Jimmy Savile inquiries. She had a calm, thoughtful presence to her. As soon as I walked into the room, she came over, shook my hand and said, Mr Lawrence. It sounds a small detail, but it immediately felt warm and respectful – a complete contrast to the coroner, who even at the inquest was still calling me Mr Lee.

At the start of the meeting, she began by giving a short speech to say exactly why we were there and what we hoped the meeting would achieve. Then she opened the floor to me.

By this point, I was used to speaking publicly, but each time I'd had to do it the stakes got that little bit higher; I was always having to take another step up, onto a higher rung of the ladder. What I mean is, I was still nervous. I'd known for a while that I'd been going to give this speech but had been racking my brains as to precisely what it was I was going to say. It was only the night before that I'd decided how to approach it.

I cleared my throat: What I want to do today is to tell you a little bit about my mum. My mum's become known as the woman who was shot by the police in Brixton that caused an uprising. But what I want you to understand today is that she was so much more than that. I need you to understand who she was as a person. I need you to understand what she meant to us.

In a folder in front of me, I had a small pile of photographs, cards and newspaper articles. I took the first one out. It was a black-and-white photograph of my mum, taken well before the shooting. She's dressed up, in a simple white dress with a string of pearls around her neck. She's looking straight at the camera: a young, confident, beautiful woman.

This is my mum, I said, holding the picture up.

The next item I pulled out of the folder was a card that I'd written to my mum one Christmas. On the front was a pair of doves, one holding some holly leaves in its mouth. The front reads: For You, Mum, with Love at Christmas. Christmas is the perfect time to let those we love the most know how important they are to us.

I explained to the room how I tried to tell my mum, in that card, exactly how I felt. I passed it to Rose to read: this wasn't a day I wanted to struggle and stumble over the words, due to my dyslexia.

'Mum,' my sister read, 'I have decided to write this letter because there are some things that I have wanted to say but could never find the right moment, and because we are not good at expressing ourselves to one another. You always tell me how proud you are of me and for what I have achieved and I am glad that I make you proud. But there is something I want you to realise. You need to be proud of yourself also because who I am and what I do is because of you.

'No matter how hard things got, and let's face it things got really hard, but Mum you never gave up and that is the biggest thing I admire about you. There are very few people who could survive your experiences and that is what makes you so special. I know you love us kids a lot and that is the main reason why you have struggled and fought for so long but Mum now I want you to stop just living for us and live for yourself. I love you a lot Mum and to see you wasting your life in the bed makes me sad. You have come too far to give up now. You deserve to be happy. Thank you for all you have done for me and for being my mum.'

The next picture I held up was of me as a young boy. I explained to the room how, when I was young, I'd wanted to be a policeman.

Then I showed them a newspaper article. SHOT IN FRONT OF HER KIDS was the headline. Underneath was the picture that the journalist had taken of me and my sisters on our sofa that morning. I described the aftermath of the shooting, how the house had been full of policemen, dogs, how this photographer had come in and taken the photo of us, in our most vulnerable moment.

I pulled out another newspaper article. COURT ORDEAL FOR SHOT MUM. This was a picture of my mum in her wheel-chair, being pushed into the Old Bailey by her brother Mervin, to hear the trial of Inspector Lovelock. I told the room about the trial, about how unfair it had felt and seemed, and our reaction to the ruling. I talked, too, about my mum's adjustment to life in a wheelchair. And how we, as children, had tried our best to support her.

The next photo was one of my mum in hospital, when she only had a few days left to live. It was a hard photo for me to look at. In the picture she's lying there, eyes closed, wired up to various machines, one tube going into her mouth, another into her nose. I talked about her passing, and the effect that it had had on our family.

I showed them another newspaper article. This was of the campaign to get legal aid so we could have representation in the inquest process. The photo was of the family and our MP, Chuka Umunna, on the steps of 10 Downing Street. I explained about the petition, how we'd gathered over 130,000 signatures and managed to get the original decision refusing legal aid overturned, which in turn had allowed us to go into the inquest on an equal footing.

The final thing I had to show was a simple one. It was a picture of my daughter Harmony, stood to attention and looking up at the camera in her school uniform. It's a photo of her that always melts my heart: she's got her hair in pigtails and has this beautiful gappy smile from where her teeth are coming through. I said how I'd found her reading a school book about the police, and how I was torn about what to tell her. That I wanted my daughter to grow up to do right and be law-abiding, that I didn't want to undermine her attitude towards the police. But how difficult it was to square that with my own experiences.

I don't want the residue of what has happened to us, the trauma and injustice, to live on in the next generation, I said, holding up Harmony's photo. The only way we can guarantee that is if we end this today. I want us to take that opportunity. I believe the opportunity is now.

I put the photo down alongside the others in the middle of the table. Four photos. Three articles. One Christmas card. A lifetime.

I wasn't really sure what would happen next, but I was expecting some kind of challenge from them, as that was what I had become accustomed to. To my surprise, it didn't come. I glanced over at the mediator, who in turn looked over to Neil Basu. He stood up. His cheeks were red, I could see. His eyes, too, looked a little glossy.

My lawyers aren't going to like what I'm going to say, Neil began, his voice cracking a little around the edges. But I just want to say that I would hate for my mum to have gone through what your mum went through. I don't know if I would have been able to deal with it in the way that you have.

This, in many ways, was the key moment in the whole process. It was the moment where I thought: *finally, the police understand.* Neil's response was a human one – person to person. It was the moment when we felt equal, on that most basic level, connecting and understanding. Irrespective of the fact that we were sat on opposite sides of the table, he was in a uniform and I wasn't, we were both sons. And that was the moment it felt like our case had cut through.

One of his lawyers reached out towards the picture of my mum as a young woman.

May I? he asked. I nodded and he picked it up and stared at it. Your mother was a beautiful woman, he said, placing it back down in front of him.

Thank you, I thought.

Another of the lawyers took the card that I had written to my mum. He started asking questions about that – how old I was when I wrote it, how old my mum would have been at the time. A third lawyer asked if they could borrow the photographs to take with them while they were deliberating.

Of course, I said, gesturing outwards with my palms to say, *Please do.*

You've given us a lot to think about, Neil said. And, trust me, we will be taking on board everything that you've said.

Trust me. After everything that had happened to us over the decades, those felt like two small but loaded words. But as Neil and I looked at each other, as I saw that tearing-up in his eyes, for the first time I thought to myself, *You know what? This time, maybe I can.*

Thirty-Eight

It really never was about the money, but the Met came back with a settlement offer which was practically double what we'd been offered in advance of the meeting. More importantly, it was part of a package of measures that we agreed in the mediation meetings.

The first of these was for a commitment that the Metropolitan Police support the Cherry Groce Foundation, which we as a family had set up. Together with their support, we built a memorial for our mum to both celebrate who she was and also to allow the community to remember her and what happened to her. You can visit that memorial in Windrush Square in Brixton. It was designed by the world-renowned architect Sir David Adjaye. The design is simple, elegant and captivating: it uses triangles to symbolise the mountains of West Africa and Jamaica that formed my mum's heritage, and it has a thick central pillar, to give a sense of strength and support. The Foundation is also working to put together a programme of teaching and educational resources that schools across the country can use to tell students about our mum's story, to think about the ideas of justice and history, and to enable and empower them on these issues as they go forwards in life themselves.

The Met also agreed that they would set up an award in our mum's name. This will be given to a member of the police force who does outstanding work within the community. The idea is that the award will push excellence and better practice, and that by celebrating that in Mum's name, the police will be reminded about what happened, and this in turn will spur them on to improve and do better.

There are further conversations around input into the training of police officers; I'd like to speak to recruits about my experiences, and maybe go on away-days with more senior officers to discuss the case. We are also looking at setting up a restorative justice process, so police officers who are on a warning about insensitive or racist behaviour can be enlightened about the effects of their actions and how they impact on people – in the same sort of way that you can do those speed awareness courses when you get a speeding ticket. In addition, we propose to set up a programme for victims who have experienced trauma at the hands of the police.

In Lord Scarman's report on the 1981 Brixton uprising, he set out what he felt were the two core principles of policing: the first of these was consent and balance; the second was independence and accountability. The independence of the police is crucial in a free society. But if their judgement is questioned, then it can lose the support of the community it has been set up to protect. The way to make sure that the police maintain that support is through accountability. If the police are accountable for their actions, then trust in their independence is maintained. If they're not, then that trust can fast become eroded.

That, for me, was what this latter part of the process had been about. Without accountability, the authority of the police is worthless. And although the Met fought hard at first over the issue, in the mediation process I felt that they finally understood. Once we got past the legal stuff and reparation, the discussion became something much more fundamental: about what job the police were there to do, and how it functioned as a force. If the police respect the community, the community respect the police: simple as. That wasn't the case in either direction in Brixton in the 1980s. For the police to belatedly accept proper accountability for their actions is a step in the right direction. Time will tell.

For all the changes in policing since the 1980s, there remains a long way for them still to go. Back in 1981, Lord Scarman had flagged up the issue of police recruitment in his report on the Brixton uprising: 'there is widespread agreement that the composition of our police forces must reflect the make-up of the society they serve. In the police, as in other important areas of society, the ethnic minorities are very significantly under-represented.'

He noted that the number of Black officers serving in the Metropolitan Police at the time was just 132, 0.5 per cent of the force. He called for 'vigorous action' to change this, noting, 'A police force which fails to reflect the ethnic diversity of our society will never succeed in securing the full support of all its sections.'

In 1999, the Macpherson report into the death of Stephen Lawrence offered a series of recommendations to help improve openness, accountability and the restoration of confidence. It wanted what it called a ministerial policy to be established across police services, to 'increase trust and confidence in policing amongst minority ethnic communities'. This policy included setting up performance indicators on issues such as the number of recorded racist incidents, satisfaction levels across all ethnic groups, and the levels of recruitment, retention and progression of minority ethnic recruits. 'The Home Office and Police Authorities should seek to ensure that the membership of police authorities reflect so far as possible the cultural and ethnic mix of the communities which those authorities serve,' Macpherson wrote.

However, in early 2020, a study by the Police Foundation thinktank found that the number of Black police officers had barely risen in recent years. Between 2007 and 2018 the number of Black police officers across England and Wales rose by just eighty-six officers – an average annual increase of eight officers a year across the entire country. Eight.

In 2007, the number of Black officers in the police force totalled 1412 or 1 per cent of the total force; in 2018, that figure was 1498 or 1.2 per cent (this lack of increase partly reflects an overall reduction in the number of police officers over the same period). In terms of the Metropolitan Police area specifically (all of London, bar the City of London area) the latest figures show that while 13.3 per cent of the population is Black, just 3.5 per cent of its police officers are; and while the population there is 59.8 per cent white, its police force is 85 per cent so.

Changing this is not easy. As Ian Hopkins, the Chief of Greater Manchester Police, said in early 2020, 'The slower rate of progress in recruiting Black police officers is likely to reflect the fact that confidence in police has historically been lower among Black people than white or Asian.' It's a bit of a chicken-and-egg situation: you need more Black police officers to increase confidence in the Black community, but you need more confidence in the Black community to encourage its members to become police officers.

Those from the Black community who have joined the police force have challenges on both sides: Scarman said in his report that 'I have heard evidence that when Black officers do join the police, they are treated with open hostility and contempt by at least some members of their own community.'

Michael Fuller, who rose to become Britain's first Black chief constable in 2004, described his experiences of going through the ranks in his memoir, *Kill the Black One First*. The title of his book came from a shout when he was one of the officers sent to deal with the Brixton uprising in 1981. Fuller talks about the challenge of joining the force: the casual racism and comments from his colleagues he had to put up with; the ongoing suspicions that he got preferential treatment because of the colour of his skin.

Like Scarman's comments, Fuller's experiences are primarily from the 1980s rather than the present day. But as those recruitment figures show, there remains a long way to go to make the police force reflective of the country we live in.

Thirty-Nine

After the mediations had ended, Sir Bernard Hogan-Howe invited Lisa and me to his office. Unlike after the inquest, when he'd read out the lawyer-approved apology to us in his crisp uniform, this time he was dressed down, and we all sat on sofas.

The reason I've asked you here today, he said, is because I'd like to invite you along to the passing out of our new recruits. My last passing out, as it happens. You'll be there as my guests, and it'll give you an idea, I hope, of where we're at now with our policing and recruitment.

I could see from the way that he was offering that he was genuine about this, and that he was making a real effort to reach out. I still had my reservations due to my past experiences, but after serious consideration, I accepted, as I felt that if I wanted to make a real difference, I first needed to understand how current policing worked.

The Met's training centre is up at Hendon, in north London. It has recently been redeveloped, with the new buildings a modern mix of black and glass, and a strip of that emergency-services shade of bright yellow across the top. Robyn Williams, a senior officer, gave us the tour, showing us around the new facilities. We were then given the best seats for the parade, where the new recruits line up in front of the Commissioner, other senior police officers and their friends and family. For those passing out, it's a big day.

The recruits stood to attention in their black uniforms, white shirts and black ties, the police badges on their helmets glistening in the sunshine. The Commissioner gave a speech. In it he introduced us and explained who we were and why we were there. He spoke of what we'd done in campaigning for Mum, and the audience applauded us. The applause filled us up. It was a powerful, moving moment. I'd been wary beforehand of whether I should go; I hadn't wanted to be used as a publicity exercise for the Met. Instead it felt as if he was teaching the next generation of police officers, which was so aligned with what I'd wanted out of the mediation process.

I wanted to know more about the system and how these recruits were trained. One of the things that struck me was just how young they were. Looking out at that sea of faces, the callowness of these new recruits stood out. Barely out of their teens and here they were, passed to go out on the street with the power to enforce law and order. If you think about what you were like at that age, what little you knew about the world, that's a scary prospect.

There was a rawness there, of young, impressionable minds. How does someone like that deal with a situation out on the streets? A lot of the time, recruits are coming from outside of London. Depending on where they've come from, they might not have had much contact with people of colour growing up: what they know is what they've been told or seen in the media. I talked to one recruit about his training and asked whether he was taught any negotiation skills, like how to mediate in a situation. He said no.

We're taught to assume, he said.

I got that there was a logic behind this. In a dangerous situation, you've got to be able to make a quick decision and go with your instincts, runs the theory. Stopping to think might get you hurt, or worse. But making assumptions about people, that's a dangerous thing to do in a different way. If you're putting people in situations where they don't know the place, don't know the culture, what sort of assumptions are those raw police officers going to make? In some cultures, it can be normal for people to speak loudly to each other – if you don't know that, are you going to misread that interaction?

I came away thinking that if you're being sent into certain communities, then you need to be given some sort of awareness training beforehand. The more you know what that community is like, the more you understand them and the better the policing, surely. If assumptions are part of the police training, then you should at least make sure that those assumptions are accurate ones.

I asked some of the recruits why they had decided to become police officers. I got good and interesting answers back. There was a lot of eagerness and enthusiasm in there. It reminded me again how different people can be in the same organisation, and the danger of blanketing everyone the same way. How, I wondered, did the system encourage these people and keep that positivity and yearning to do good going? How did it find out if there were bad apples and mould them to be good? How do you stop that beginner's enthusiasm being soured by the I've-seen-it-all attitude down at the station?

When I'd finished talking to some of the recruits, I turned around to a mixed-race officer who I'd seen had been waiting to talk to me. To my surprise, she reached over and hugged me and Lisa.

She was crying. I just wanted you to know, she said. That it was because of what happened to your family that I became a police officer.

I was really taken aback. I'd assumed that our family's story would have made people less likely to join the police. But here, in fact, the opposite was the case. This woman didn't want what had happened to our family to happen to someone else's. I was humbled by this.

After refreshments and further conversations, it was time to leave. As I said goodbye to the Commissioner, he said, Thank you for coming. I wondered whether you might have brought your daughter with you.

I smiled. Clearly the presentation that I'd made at the mediation meeting had got back to him. But in my head I was thinking, *Hell, no way. I'm not convinced yet.*

I want my children to feel they can trust the police, that though the police behaved badly towards us in the past, they've accepted responsibility for that and want to do better in the future. When my daughters are grown up they can choose for themselves what career paths they want to follow. I would support the career paths any of my children choose to follow, however right now, because of my own personal experiences, I can't actively encourage one within the police service. Maybe one day, and I would love to see that day, but not yet.

Things are changing. That day at the passing out parade, while the majority of the new recruits were white, I was encouraged to see some Black and Asian officers among them – more than I was expecting. I would never discourage others from applying, because it's important for our community to have proper representation in the police service; I truly believe that. But as well as that representation, which I feel would lead to a better relationship between the police and the community they serve, institutional racism within it also needs to be dealt with. When racial minorities make that important choice to join the police, they should feel they have just as much chance to climb the ladder as everyone else.

In November 2019, the superintendent who had been tasked with giving us a tour of the new facilities at the passing out parade – Robyn Williams – was convicted of being in possession of a child abuse video. The video had been sent to her unsolicited by her sister, who wanted the person behind it arrested. Even though it was proved in court that Williams hadn't opened the video, the fact it existed on her phone was enough to convict her. She was sentenced to two hundred hours of unpaid work, was added to the sex offenders' register and put on restricted duties at work, with no contact with the public.

Williams's record of over thirty-six years with the police had been exemplary. She had won awards and was lauded for her work in the aftermath of the Grenfell fire. The Black Police Association said afterwards that the Met had the discretion not to pursue Williams but had decided to do so anyway. They accused the Met of 'a classic example of institutional racism ... there have been many examples in the last couple of years of Black senior officers being held to account at a higher level than their white counterparts. This has to stop.'

There was also shock and anger within the Black community at how she had been treated. In terms of persuading people to sign up for the police force, cases like this don't make recruitment any easier.

There are good people in the police, fighting for the changes that need to be made. But they can't achieve them by themselves. They need government support to be able to do that, to make those changes permanent for my children's generation, and for those beyond as well.

Forty

If the police is a force, it should be a force for good. I want to help that happen.

Beyond the work of the Cherry Groce Foundation, I sit on the advisory board of various police departments in Brixton as a member of the community, helping to advise the police about their behaviour and tactics. In Brixton, I've been in meetings where the local commander has asked our opinion on what their priorities should be: they were asking the community what we felt they should be focusing on. That might not sound like much, but it's those sorts of meetings that help to build relationships between the police and the community – meetings that were entirely absent back in the early 1980s.

I also sit on an advisory board of Scotland Yard. This has been brought together to look at issues such as police behaviour, professional standards and how the force deals with the public, and any issues of misconduct that might arise. This is an area that I'm passionate about. If I can use my experiences to help improve policing, then it feels as though my own personal journey will have been worthwhile.

I've also trained to become a mediator. Reflecting on it afterwards, the mediation process both impressed and inspired me.

Even though the family had had a voice in the inquest, it was a structured process: you came in, you did your specific part, you went away. With the mediation, however, you sat face to face with the people you wanted to talk to. We were able to really speak, to put our point across as we wanted to, and to be heard. Being able to do so was incredibly therapeutic and part of our healing process.

The mediation course I signed up for was at Regent's University. It wasn't a very diverse group doing the course and the majority were from the legal profession: lawyers, barristers, even judges. On that first day, I think I was the only Black person in the room. But the funny thing was that, for all of their qualifications, a number of the lawyers struggled with the course. Mediation is a different sort of skill. Rather than being the one in control and putting your own arguments forward, mediating is about sitting back and using softer skills. By contrast, it turned out that these softer skills were exactly what I had.

You are what we'd call a natural mediator, my tutor told me during one feedback session. That felt quite an empowering moment. I might not have had the qualifications to match any of the other students, but I had the instinctive skills.

After getting my qualifications to be able to mediate, I then went on and did a further course in restorative justice, this time with an organisation called Calm Mediation. Mediation is normally a process without right or wrong – you deal with two competing views that you're trying to reconcile or reach some sort of compromise between. With restorative justice, the difference between the two parties is clear: one is the perpetrator, the other the victim. It's a process where these two sides can come together. For the perpetrator, it's a chance to face up to what they've done and understand the consequences of their actions. For the victim, it's a chance to speak to the perpetrator, to find out why they behaved as they did. In the language of restorative justice, it would be referred to as the harmer and the harmed.

The process can be beneficial in all sorts of ways. For the perpetrator, it offers the possibility of a shorter sentence or earlier release if they agree to take part in the programme. In terms of reoffending, criminals who have taken part in a restorative justice process are less likely to offend again. For the victim, it is an opportunity to ask the perpetrator questions directly, and gives them a sense of understanding and closure they might not otherwise have had. For the police, it has the potential to lead to a reduction in crime rates and reduce the number of people going to prison. Some of the cases I learned about on the course are extraordinary: there was one in the United States, where a woman's son was shot by another boy. She visited the boy in jail as part of the process. When the boy was eventually released, she ended up putting him up in her home. When she realised what he had been through and the trauma he had suffered, she knew that, in a way, he was just as much of a victim as her son was.

There has been a recent drive in London to encourage people to use the restorative justice process more, particularly in areas such as youth offending and probation, around an initiative called Restore London. I'm looking forward to getting involved in this area of work.

Forty-One

My dad died in February 2020.

During my teenage years, whatever relationship I'd had with him began to melt away. Instead of spending weekends with him we'd meet in a pub, Lisa and I sipping Pepsi or lemonade as he drank his beer. He wouldn't ask us questions about what we'd been up to or how school was; he'd sit with his head in the newspaper.

Very occasionally, he'd ring home and my mum would say, Oh, Leo called. He's coming over on Saturday.

But I wouldn't go out of my way to be there, and would sometimes even see it as convenient not to be.

Afterwards, Mum would tell me off: But you knew he was coming.

And I'd respond, Why should I break my neck to be here, when he decides to come here once a year?

One of the last times he came to see my mum, I was there. I didn't want to go through the same conversation again, so I simply asked him, Have you had any regrets in your life?

I could tell from his reaction that he was caught a little off guard by that. I knew what I wanted his answer to be, but after a pause he said, No, not many. I did a lot of travelling when I was in the army. But maybe I wish I travelled more, outside of that.

Later, after I'd gone, he told my mum that he really didn't like being asked that question, that I shouldn't have put him in that position. But I thought, *You know what? That was such a polite way of asking what I really wanted to ask, and if you're not going to begin to respond to that, then there's no point taking this further.* And so I gave up there and then on trying to have a more meaningful relationship and accepted things for what they were.

In more recent years, every Christmas I'd invite my dad to come and spend it with me, Gem and the girls. He never came, but that was OK – I got used to that over the years, but still wanted him to know that the door was always open.

In December 2019, I called him to make my usual invitation. But this time he didn't answer the phone. Lisa was concerned and went over to see him. She was shocked by how much of a struggle it was for him to get to the door. He wasn't well at all.

In the run-up to Christmas, Lisa and I took turns to see him. He'd lost weight and developed a cough. He'd always smoked a lot – he said it was just a smoker's cough. By Christmas it was worse. Lisa had gone to visit him and on seeing him, insisted on calling an ambulance.

It transpired that my father had not only been diagnosed with cancer, but that the cancer was terminal: the doctors had given him just months to live. My dad was initially in denial about it, but it got to the point that he couldn't ignore it and needed medical attention.

My feelings on the diagnosis stirred up a mixture of emotions. My heart went out to him, for what he must have been going through. I was worried for him and what would lie ahead. But equally, part of me thought that he'd done this to himself through all his years of heavy drinking and smoking. I couldn't help thinking about what we'd missed out on, and what we would miss out on as a family because of that. That sense of waste and frustration was in there for me. With the clock ticking down, it reinforced how I'd never really got to know him as a person. And that wasn't just me and Lisa, it was my children, too, who he had never really had a proper relationship with, and now never would. But, after all was said and done, he was my father and I was going to care for him and be there for him.

While we still had time, I had questions. One day, when Lisa and I sat next to his bed in St Thomas' Hospital, perched on those familiar plastic hospital chairs, I got Lisa to ask the question I wanted to hear him answer. Why had he always insisted that we call him Leo rather than Dad? The hospital had made that starker: the nurses would quiz us about who we were because we weren't calling him Dad, saying the visiting was only for close relatives.

My dad's response was that it wasn't unusual, and a lot of people called their parents by their real names. I asked him if he'd done that.

No, my dad replied. He'd called his parents Mum and Dad.

We sat there for a minute, and then I asked him if he remembered the day that Lisa and I tried to call him Dad. It was a memory that remains seared in my mind, as fresh as if it happened yesterday. But my dad just looked blankly at me as I described it. He had no recollection of that evening at all.

On another occasion, I brought with me some photos that I'd found when I'd been in his flat collecting some stuff he'd asked us to bring. They were of him in the army – pictures I'd never seen before and a part of his life that he'd never really talked about to us. I asked him about that, and whether he'd ever risen through the ranks. I know that there were other Black soldiers at the time who'd done so. My dad said that he hadn't, out of choice, that he didn't want the responsibility. It suddenly made so much sense.

The next time Lisa and I went to see him, he had a wary look in his eye.

Are you here to interrogate me again? he asked. What questions have you got for me today?

I shook my head. I didn't want him to feel under pressure if he wasn't well.

Are you bothered by it, us asking you questions? I said.

Now it was his turn to shake his head, though I could tell he felt ruffled and a bit on edge about it.

You're spending a lot of time here, he said. It must be having an impact on all your other work.

I was surprised by that comment, but also touched. It was unusual for him to recognise what I did, and it was nice to know that he'd been thinking about that. A small detail, perhaps, but it felt significant.

On 15 February 2020, I was woken at six in the morning. Gem told me Lisa had called to say the hospital had rung. They said we should go straight down there. I had that funny familiar feeling I remembered from when Mum was in hospital.

By the time I met Lisa at the hospital, my dad had stopped breathing. I hugged him. His body was still warm. As Lisa and I said our goodbyes with a prayer, I found myself full of emotion in a way that caught me off guard. I'd never had a particularly close relationship with my father, but that connection in that moment, the way I was able to grieve his passing, it meant a lot.

Whenever it is my mum's birthday, we try to get together as a family, as our way of remembering her.

If the sun is shining, then I'll invite everyone round to ours for a barbecue. We do things to remind us of Mum. Play a game of dominoes, which she used to love. Get the jerk chicken cooking. Ramp up the music.

As I turn over the drumsticks, hissing and spitting on the rack, I'll watch the family spread out across the lawn in front of me. My wife and my children. My sisters. Nieces and nephews. I always think to myself, *She would have been proud of this scene, and how we've all ended up in our different ways.* There's Lisa, now an assistant nurse at St George's Hospital in Tooting. Rose, whose patience and care

260

with children has led to a career in nannying. Sharon, who has been bitten by the travel bug, and is always full of tales about her latest trip to Jamaica or Barbados or the Gambia.

As for me, I have jobs that are meaningful and that I'm invested in. If you'd told that eleven-year-old boy back in 1985 where he'd be today, he wouldn't have believed it. Life is about losing yourself, then finding yourself. For a while, I lost myself in the alter egos that I created. Rudy Lee, the young MC. Younger Cowboy, the bad guy. Brandy Lee, the life and soul of the party. Somehow, I've managed to go full circle. I've learned that I'm strongest when I am in tune to my authentic self. Just Lee.

Now I can engage properly with the police. I can sit on their advisory boards and look at how we can work to improve their practices. I've been able to begin my own healing process and, by learning to mediate and by training in restorative justice, I'm ready to try to inspire and encourage others.

The next chapter of my life is about to begin. I'm looking forward to seeing where it might take me.

Epilogue

My mum will always be remembered as the woman who was shot by police in her own home, the trigger for the 1985 Brixton uprising. But that wasn't who she was. Being our mum wasn't even who she was. She had her own identity, her own spirit, her own fire. Let me tell you a bit about her.

She was from Jamaica and it burned in her. Her accent was laced with it, the sound of the waves in the rolls of her 'r's. In the house in Gipsy Hill, her brother Tony, also known as Mooji now, painted murals of the sweeping waterfalls that fell in the Blue Mountains, the backdrop to her childhood.

She was a Maroon. The word comes from the Spanish *cimarròn*, meaning wild. The term referred to those slaves in the seventeenth and eighteenth centuries who escaped and set about starting a new life of their own, either in their own communities or by becoming part of a local indigenous group. Evading recapture was a high-risk endeavour. Anyone caught knew that the punishment meted out to them was likely to be severe, as a warning to others.

In Jamaica, the story of the Maroons was more complicated than elsewhere in the Americas and Caribbean. The island had originally been seized by the Spanish, and it was their slaves who first escaped and started their own communities in the mountains.

In 1655, when the British invaded, these numbers were swelled by those left behind by the departing Spanish. The British, meanwhile, brought in their own slaves in increasing numbers to do plantation work. As some of these slaves escaped to join the Maroon communities, the British attempts to stop them led to two Maroon wars in the eighteenth century, both of which ended inconclusively: the British were by far the stronger military force, but the Maroons' knowledge of the land and the mountains they lived in cancelled out this advantage. In the end, the government agreed to the Maroons' right to land and autonomy, in return for peace.

One of the most prominent Maroon leaders in Jamaica was known as Nanny of the Maroons, or sometimes Nanny Granny. Nanny was born in Ghana and there are differing stories as to how she ended up in Jamaica – one version says she was an escapee, jumping ship as her slave ship arrived in Jamaica, another that she was always free and ended up on the island of her own accord. What isn't disputed is that she was incredibly skilful when it came to military strategy: she was one of the leaders from the First Maroon War of 1720–39. Nanny was an inspirational figure, not just for her leadership, but also because she continued the customs and culture of her African ancestors.

Those were the customs and cultures my mum grew up with, bred in her bones. In her town was a community corporal – an echo of the West African tradition where you have an elder or a chief – who knows everyone and everything. When I went out to Jamaica after my mum died, the corporal, now in his nineties, still remembered her.

God, she could cook, and no matter what ingredients she had, she could bring them to life with paprika or pepper, thyme or garlic. When I was older she explained to me the history behind some of the dishes: that a number of them originated from when our people had been slaves, and had to make do with the worst parts of an animal, the bits that no one else wanted to eat, but how with spices you could make anything palatable. Meals were family occasions; she'd want us all to sit around the table and feel the love she'd put into preparing the food in front of us.

She was brave. She was the oldest of her eight siblings. My gran came over to England from Jamaica in the 1950s, and when my mum was fifteen she joined her – leaving behind the rest of her family and her home to travel 4649 miles to start a new life.

She loved deeply, and my father most of all. She met him at the Angel, one of the Black pubs in Brixton at the time. She was introduced to him by a guy called Trevor, who was in the army with my dad. He pronounced her name Sherry, rather than Cherry. He treated her like a lady, bought her flowers, chocolates and records. He had a way about him, my mum explained, the way he carried himself. He was neat and sharp, that little bit of the army in him in how his shoes were always polished and how he was well turned out. And she loved us, her children, saving her money to give us the things we needed instead of the things she did.

I asked my sisters what they remembered when they thought of Mum. She loved a good laugh, Lisa recalled. Whenever any one of us did or said something funny she would laugh so much her eyes would water. Juliet said, The many things that I will always miss and remember her for are her knowledge, insight and wisdom about what is really going on in the world today. Sharon remembered the time we moved to Gipsy Hill and spent that first night there sleeping on the carpet. Rose recollected the time she was ten or eleven and really wanted a sewing machine. Mum couldn't afford it, she said. Then one day she won some money at the betting shop and spent her winnings buying it for me. I was so happy.

When I picture Mum, it's her face when she peeled 'Someone Loves You Honey' out from its sleeve. The satisfying crackle as the needle touched the outer edge of the record, and then the music started. She swayed in time to the rhythm, between the sofa and the coffee table, and she encouraged us to get up with her, and we all danced around her, our maypole, our matriarch.

That's how I think of her now.

Dancing, always dancing.

Postscript

17 July 2020

On the evening of 25 May 2020, Minneapolis police responded to a call from a branch of Cup Foods grocery store in the city. The shop assistant claimed that a customer had bought a packet of cigarettes with a counterfeit $20 bill. The customer in question was forty-six-year-old George Floyd.

What happened next would result in an unprecedented global response to police brutality and lead to ongoing debate about racism throughout society. Filmed by passers-by on their mobile phones, George Floyd was pinned to the ground by a white police officer, Derek Chauvin. Despite Floyd saying more than twenty times that he couldn't breathe, Chauvin kept his knee pressed on Floyd's neck for almost nine minutes. He was taken immediately to hospital by ambulance, where he was pronounced dead.

Watching the footage, the first trigger for me was when Floyd said those three tragic words. *I can't breathe.* The sight of a white officer in an overpowering position over a Black person took me straight back to 22 Normandy Road. Mum lying on the floor. Lovelock towering over her. *This is madness*, I thought. That this was happening not just in 2020, but in the middle of a pandemic. Even when the world had

267

stopped, police brutality against the Black community still continued. The fact that Floyd was forty-six and I turned forty-six a couple of months later, that hit home in the same way Stephen Lawrence's murder had affected me in my early twenties.

But while I was shocked to see how little had changed since Stephen's murder, and the shooting of my mum, I also took heart from the resulting Black Lives Matter protests. I spoke to someone who'd been on both the protests after Mum was shot and the George Floyd marches. Back in 1985, he said, any white person on a march would stick out like a sore thumb. Today, the mixture of people protesting was completely different and from right across society. And younger, too. That felt generational. That felt different.

I went on one of the protest marches to the US Embassy in Vauxhall. I took my two daughters. I wanted them to understand who we are, where we've come from, who their grandmother was and why her case still mattered. We were careful: we had gloves on, wore masks, and didn't venture into the thick of the action. Once I felt they'd got a sense of the protests, we headed home.

Homemade placards were everywhere. *Black Lives Matter. Racism is a Virus. The UK Is Not Innocent.* On some signs, people had written the names of people who had suffered at the hands of the police. Mark Duggan. Sean Rigg. Joy Gardner. Cherry Groce ... When I saw Mum's name among them, I felt humbled. That people still remembered her and what happened, that meant a lot.

Will the protests lead to permanent change? Instinctively, I would say yes, it does feel as though a shift has occurred. But thinking back about my own experiences, I'm much more cautious. What I do know is that it's not enough to think things will just happen: we've got to keep applying the pressure to make sure that change is permanent.

None of this is easy. None of this is a quick fix. But in a year when statues to slave-traders are torn down and a memorial to my mum is put up, now feels as good a time as any to make a start.